MICHIGAN NONPROFIT CORPORATION ACT
2016 Edition

Updated through January 1, 2016

I0476824

Michigan Legal Publishing Ltd.
QUICK DESK REFERENCE SERIES™

Academic and bulk discounts available at
www.michlp.com

No claim to copyright of any government works. While we efforts to ensure this text is accurate, there is no guarantee that the rules and statutes in this publication are the latest and most up-to-date. Accordingly, this text is for educational purposes only and should not be considered legal advice.

WE WELCOME YOUR FEEDBACK: info@michlp.com

PLEASE NOTE: The chapter titles are added by the publisher and should not be considered a part of the statute text.

ISBN-13: 978-1522895558
ISBN-10: 1522895558

NONPROFIT CORPORATION ACT
Act 162 of 1982

AN ACT to revise, consolidate, and classify the laws relating to the organization and regulation of certain nonprofit corporations; to prescribe their duties, rights, powers, immunities, and liabilities; to provide for the authorization of foreign nonprofit corporations within this state; to impose certain duties on certain state departments; to prescribe fees; to prescribe penalties for violations of this act; and to repeal certain acts and parts of acts.

The People of the State of Michigan enact:

Chapter 1 – General Provisions

450.2101 Short title.
Sec. 101.

This act shall be known and may be cited as the "nonprofit corporation act".

450.2103 Construction and application of act.
Sec. 103.

This act shall be liberally construed and applied to promote its underlying purposes and policies which include all of the following:
(a) To simplify, clarify, and modernize the law governing nonprofit corporations.
(b) To provide a general corporate form for the conduct or promotion of lawful nonprofit activities or purposes, with any variations and modifications from the form as interested parties in any corporation may agree on, subject only to overriding interests of this state and of third parties.

450.2104 Definitions generally.
Sec. 104.

The definitions contained in sections 105 to 110 shall control the interpretation of this act, unless the context otherwise requires.

450.2105 Definitions; A, B.
Sec. 105.

(1) "Administrator" means the director of the department or his or her designated representative.
(2) "Articles of incorporation" includes any of the following:

   (a) The original articles of incorporation or any other instrument filed or issued under any statute to organize a domestic or foreign corporation, as amended, supplemented, or restated by certificates of amendment, merger, conversion, or consolidation, or other certificates or instruments filed or issued under any statute.

   (b) A special act or charter creating a domestic or foreign corporation, as amended, supplemented, or restated.

(3) "Authorized shares" means shares of all classes that a corporation is authorized to issue.

(4) "Ballot" means an instrument in written or electronic form that is designed to record the vote or votes of shareholders or members under section 408 or section 409 or at a meeting of the shareholders or members.

(5) "Board" means board of directors or trustees or other governing board of a corporation.

(6) "Bonds" includes secured and unsecured bonds, debentures, and notes.

(7) "Business corporation" or "domestic business corporation" means a corporation for profit formed under the business corporation act, or existing on January 1, 1973 and formed before January 1, 1973 under any other statute of this state for a purpose for which a corporation for profit may be organized under that statute.

(8) "Business corporation act" means the business corporation act, 1972 PA 284, MCL 450.1101 to 450.2098.

450.2106 Definitions; C to E.
Sec. 106.

(1) "Charitable purpose corporation" means a domestic corporation that meets any of the following:

   (a) Is recognized by the United States internal revenue service as exempt or qualifies for exemption under section 501(c)(3) of the internal revenue code of 1986, 26 USC 501.

   (b) Is a corporation whose purposes, structure, and activities are exclusively those that are described in section 501(c)(3) of the internal revenue code of 1986, 26 USC 501.

   (c) Is a corporation organized or held out to be organized exclusively for 1 or more charitable purposes.

(2) "Corporation" or "domestic corporation" means a nonprofit corporation formed under this act, or formed under any other statute of this state and subject to this act under section 121 or 123 or under any other section of this act.

(3) "Department" means the department of licensing and regulatory affairs.

(4) "Director" means an individual who is a member of the board of a corporation. The term is synonymous with "trustee" of a corporation or other similar designation.

(5) "Distribution" means a direct or indirect transfer of money or other property, except the corporation's shares or memberships, or debt incurred by the corporation to or for the benefit of its shareholders or members in

connection with the corporation's shares or memberships. A distribution may be in the form of a dividend, a purchase, redemption or other acquisition of shares or memberships, an issuance of indebtedness, the conversion of stock or membership in the corporation to bonds or other indebtedness, or any other declaration or payment to or for the benefit of the shareholders or members.

(6) "Electronic transmission" or "electronically transmitted" means any form of communication that meets all of the following:
 (a) It does not directly involve the physical transmission of paper.
 (b) It creates a record that may be retained and retrieved by the recipient.
 (c) It may be directly reproduced in paper form by the recipient through an automated process.

450.2107 Definitions; F.
Sec. 107.

(1) "Foreign business corporation" means a corporation for profit that is formed under laws other than the laws of this state, that includes in its purposes a purpose for which a corporation may be formed under the business corporation act.
(2) "Foreign corporation" means a nonprofit corporation formed under laws other than the laws of this state, if its purpose or purposes are a purpose or purposes for which a corporation may be formed under this act.

450.2108 Definitions; M to P.
Sec. 108.

(1) "Member" means a person that has a membership in a corporation in accordance with the provisions of its articles of incorporation or bylaws.
(2) "Nonprofit corporation" means a corporation incorporated to carry out any lawful purpose or purposes that does not involve pecuniary profit or gain for its directors, officers, shareholders, or members.
(3) "Person" means an individual, a partnership, a domestic corporation, a domestic business corporation, a foreign corporation, a foreign business corporation, a limited liability company, or any other association, corporation, trust, or legal entity.
(4) "Predecessor act" means an act or part of an act repealed by this act, or an act or part of an act repealed by an act that this act repeals.
(5) "Private foundation" means a tax exempt corporation described in section 501(c)(3) of the internal revenue code of 1986, 26 USC 501, that is classified as a private foundation under section 509(a) of the internal revenue code of 1986, 26 USC 509.

450.2109 Definitions; S.
Sec. 109.
(1) "Shareholder" means a person that holds shares of a domestic corporation, foreign corporation, domestic business corporation, or foreign business corporation.
(2) "Shares" means the units into which interests of shareholders in a domestic corporation, foreign corporation, domestic business corporation, or foreign business corporation are divided.
(3) "Services in a learned profession" means services provided by a dentist, an osteopathic physician, a physician, a surgeon, a doctor of divinity or other clergy, or an attorney at law.

450.2110 Definitions; V.
Sec. 110.

(1) "Volunteer" means an individual who performs services for a corporation, other than services as a volunteer director, who does not receive compensation or any other type of consideration for the services other than reimbursement for expenses actually incurred.
(2) "Volunteer director" means a director who does not receive anything of more than nominal value from the corporation for serving as a director other than reasonable per diem compensation and reimbursement for actual, reasonable, and necessary expenses incurred by a director in his or her capacity as a director.

450.2121 Corporations to which act applicable; corporation formed under predecessor act.
Sec. 121.

(1) Except as otherwise provided in this act or by other law, this act applies to all of the following:
   (a) Every domestic corporation formed under this act or under a predecessor act, for a purpose or purposes for which a corporation might be formed under this act.
   (b) Every foreign corporation that is authorized to or does conduct affairs in this state except as otherwise provided under this act or another statute.
   (c) Any other domestic corporation or foreign corporation that is not formed under this act to the extent, if any, provided under section 123 or any other provision of this act or under a provision of any law governing that domestic or foreign corporation.
(2) A corporation formed under or subject to a predecessor act is subject to this act except to the extent that this act conflicts with the articles and bylaws of the corporation lawfully made under the predecessor act. The corporation may amend its articles and bylaws to bring itself in conformity with this act.

450.2122 Statutory reference to repealed act as reference to this act; statutes inapplicable to domestic corporation; uniform fraudulent transfer act inapplicable to distributions.
Sec. 122.

(1) A reference in any statute of this state to parts of any act that are repealed by this act is considered to be a reference to this act, unless the context requires otherwise.

(2) The following statutes do not apply to a domestic corporation:
    (a) 1846 RS 55, MCL 450.504 to 450.525.
    (b) 1955 PA 156, MCL 450.701 to 450.704.

(3) The uniform fraudulent transfer act, 1998 PA 434, MCL 566.31 to 566.43, does not apply to distributions permitted under this act.

450.2123 Applicability to corporation formed under other act not repealed by this act; organizations to which act inapplicable.
Sec. 123.

(1) Subject to subsection (3), unless otherwise provided in, and to the extent not inconsistent with, the act under which a corporation is or has been formed, this act applies to a corporation that is or has been formed under an act other than this act and not repealed by this act.

(2) A corporation described in subsection (1) includes, but is not limited to, any of the following:
    (a) A cooperative corporation classified as a nonprofit corporation under section 98 of 1931 PA 327, MCL 450.98.
    (b) A secret society or lodge.
    (c) A trustee corporation that holds property for charitable, religious, benevolent, educational, or other public benefit purposes.
    (d) A church trustee corporation.
    (e) An educational corporation that is organized as a trustee corporation or a nonprofit corporation.
    (f) An ecclesiastical corporation.
    (g) A public building corporation.
    (h) A street railway under the nonprofit street railway act, 1867 PA 35, MCL 472.1 to 472.27.

(3) Except as provided in subsection (2)(h), this act does not apply to insurance or surety companies, credit unions, savings and loan associations, fraternal benefit societies, railroad, bridge, or tunnel companies, union depot companies, or banking corporations.

450.2124 Requirements of other acts not modified; compliance; inconsistency between acts.
Sec. 124.

(1) This act does not modify the requirements of the following:

    (a) The supervision of trustees for charitable purposes act, 1961 PA 101, MCL 14.251 to 14.266.

    (b) 1965 PA 169, MCL 450.251 to 450.253.

    (c) The charitable organizations and solicitations act, 1975 PA 169, MCL 400.271 to 400.294.

    (d) The uniform prudent management of institutional funds act.

    (e) The career development and distance learning act, 2002 PA 36, MCL 390.1571 to 390.1579.

(2) A corporation subject to 1 or more of the acts listed in subsection (1) shall comply with those acts and shall comply with this act. If there is any inconsistency between those acts and this act, those acts shall control.

450.2125 Applicability to commerce with foreign nations and among several states, and to corporations formed by act of congress.
Sec. 125.

This act applies to commerce with foreign nations and among the several states and to corporations formed by or under any act of congress, only to the extent permitted under the constitution and laws of the United States.

450.2127 Effect of act on existing corporation, cause of action, liability, penalty, action, or special proceeding.
Sec. 127.

(1) Except as provided in section 261(3), this act does not affect the duration of a corporation which exists on the effective date of this act. An existing corporation and its shareholders, members, directors, and officers have the same rights and are subject to the same limitations, restrictions, liabilities, and penalties as a corporation formed under this act, and its shareholders, members, directors, and officers.

(2) This act does not affect a cause of action, liability, penalty, or action or special proceeding, which on the effective date of this act is accrued, existing, incurred, or pending, but the same may be asserted, enforced, prosecuted, or defended as if this act had not been enacted.

450.2129 Supplementation, alteration, amendment, or repeal of act by legislature.
Sec. 129.

This act may be supplemented, altered, amended, or repealed by the legislature and every corporation, domestic or foreign, to which this act applies is bound thereby.

450.2131 Submission of documents; delivery; endorsement; indexing; returning copy or original; public inspection; maintenance of records and files; reproductions; effective date of document; fees.
Sec. 131.

(1) A document required or permitted to be filed under this act shall be submitted by delivering the document to the administrator together with the fees and accompanying documents required by law. The administrator may establish a procedure for accepting delivery of a document submitted under this subsection by facsimile or by other electronic transmission. The administrator shall accept delivery of documents submitted by electronic mail or over the internet.

(2) If a document submitted under subsection (1) substantially conforms to the requirements of this act, the administrator shall endorse on it the word "filed" with his or her official title and the dates of receipt and of filing, and shall file and index the document or a reproduction of the document pursuant to the records reproduction act, 1992 PA 116, MCL 24.401 to 24.406, in his or her office. If requested at the time of the delivery of the document to the administrator's office, the administrator shall include the hour of filing in the endorsement on the document.

(3) The administrator may return a copy of a document filed under subsection (2), or, at his or her discretion, the original, to the person that submitted the document for filing. The administrator shall mark the filing date on the copy or original before returning it or may provide proof of the filing date to the person that submitted the document for filing in another manner determined by the administrator.

(4) The records and files of the administrator relating to domestic and foreign corporations shall be open to reasonable inspection by the public. The administrator may maintain the records or files either in their original form or in the form of reproductions pursuant to the records reproduction act, 1992 PA 116, MCL 24.401 to 24.406, and may destroy the original of the reproduced documents.

(5) The administrator may make reproductions of any documents filed under this act, or any predecessor act, pursuant to the records reproduction act, 1992 PA 116, MCL 24.401 to 24.406, and may destroy the originals of the reproduced documents.

(6) A document filed under subsection (2) is effective at the time it is endorsed unless a subsequent effective time, not later than 90 days after the date of delivery, is set forth in the document.

(7) The administrator shall charge 1 of the following nonrefundable fees if expedited filing of a document by the administrator is requested and the administrator shall retain the revenue collected under this subsection and the department shall use it to carry out its duties required by law:

    (a) For any filing that a person requests the administrator to complete within 1 hour on the same day as the day of the request, $1,000.00. The department may establish a deadline by which a person must submit a request for filing under this subdivision.

(b) For any filing that a person requests the administrator to complete within 2 hours on the same day as the day of the request, $500.00. The department may establish a deadline by which a person must submit a request for filing under this subdivision.

(c) Except for a filing request under subdivision (a) or (b), for the filing of any formation or qualification document that a person requests the administrator to complete on the same day as the day of the request, $100.00. The department may establish a deadline by which a person must submit a request for filing under this subdivision.

(d) Except for a filing request under subdivision (a) or (b), for the filing of any other document concerning an existing domestic corporation or a qualified foreign corporation that a person requests the administrator to complete on the same day as the day of the request, $200.00. The department may establish a deadline by which a person must submit a request for filing under this subdivision.

(e) For the filing of any formation or qualification document that a person requests the administrator to complete within 24 hours of the time the administrator receives the request, $50.00.

(f) For the filing of any other document concerning an existing domestic corporation or a qualified foreign corporation that a person requests the administrator to complete within 24 hours of the time the administrator receives the request, $100.00.

450.2132 English language; signatures; contents of documents.
Sec. 132.

(1) A document filed with the administrator shall be in the English language, except that the corporate name need not be in the English language if written in English letters or Arabic or Roman numerals.

(2) A document required or permitted to be filed under this act that is also required by this act to be executed on behalf of the domestic or foreign corporation shall be signed by an authorized officer or agent of the domestic or foreign corporation. If the board has not yet met, the document shall be signed by the incorporator or a majority of incorporators if there are more than 1. If the domestic or foreign corporation is in the hands of a receiver, trustee, or other court appointed officer, the document shall be signed by the fiduciary or a majority of the fiduciaries, if there are more than 1. The name of a person signing the document and the capacity in which he or she signs shall be stated beneath or opposite his or her signature. The document may, but need not, contain any of the following:

(a) The corporate seal.

(b) An attestation by the secretary or an assistant secretary of the corporation.

(c) An acknowledgment or proof.

450.2133 Correction of document; certificate; effective date of corrected document.
Sec. 133.

If a document relating to a domestic or foreign corporation that is filed with the administrator under this act was at the time of filing an inaccurate record of the corporation action referred to in the document or was defectively or erroneously executed, or the document was electronically transmitted and the electronic transmission was defective, the document may be corrected by filing with the administrator a certificate of correction on behalf of the corporation. A certificate entitled "certificate of correction of... (correct title of document and name of corporation)" shall be signed as provided in this act with respect to the document being corrected and filed with the administrator. The certificate shall set forth the name of the corporation, the date the document to be corrected was filed by the administrator, the provision in the document as it should have originally appeared, and if the execution was defective, the proper execution. The corrected document is effective in its corrected form as of its original filing date except as to a person that relied on the inaccurate portion of the document and was, as a result of the inaccurate portion of the document, adversely affected by the correction.

450.2141 Taking action without notice and without lapse of prescribed period of time; waiver.
Sec. 141.

If, under this act or the articles of incorporation or bylaws of a corporation or by the terms of an agreement or instrument, a corporation or the board or any committee of the board may take action after notice to any person or after lapse of a prescribed period of time, the action may be taken without notice and without lapse of the period of time, if at any time before or after the action is completed the person entitled to notice or to participate in the action to be taken or, in case of a shareholder or member, by his or her attorney-in-fact, submits a signed waiver or a waiver by electronic transmission of the requirements.

450.2142 Dispensing with notice or communication to person with whom communication unlawful; affidavit, certificate, or other instrument.
Sec. 142.

When a notice or communication is required to be given to a person by this act, by the articles of incorporation or bylaws, or by the terms of an agreement or instrument relating to the internal affairs of the corporation, or as a condition precedent to taking corporate action, and communication with the person is then unlawful under a statute of this state or the United States or a rule, regulation, proclamation, or order issued under any of those statutes, the giving of the notice or communication to the person is not required and there is no duty to apply for a license or other permission to do so. An affidavit, certificate or other instrument which is required to be made or filed as proof of the giving of a notice or communication required by this act, if the notice or communication to any person is dispensed with under this section, shall include a statement that the notice or communication was not given to any person with whom communication is unlawful. The affidavit, certificate or other instrument is as effective for all purposes as though the notice or communication had been personally given to the person.

450.2143 Giving notice or communication by mail; electronic transmission as written notice; delivery of notice or documents to common address; delivery of notice to resident agent; "address" defined.
Sec. 143.

(1) If a notice or communication is required or permitted by this act to be given by mail, it shall be mailed, except as otherwise provided in this act, to the person to which it is directed at the address designated by that person for that purpose or, if none is designated, at that person's last known address. The notice or communication is given when deposited, with postage prepaid, in a post office or official depository under the exclusive care and custody of the United States postal service. The mailing shall be sent by registered, certified, or other first class mail unless otherwise required under this act.

(2) If a notice is required or permitted by this act to be given in writing, electronic transmission is written notice.

(3) If a corporation is required or permitted to provide its shareholders or members with a written notice or other written report, statement, or communications under this act, the articles of incorporation, or the bylaws, the corporation may provide that notice, report, statement, or communication to all shareholders or members that share a common address by delivering 1 copy of it to the common address if all of the following are met:

   (a) The corporation addresses the notice, report, statement, or communication to the shareholders or members that share the common address as a group, individually, or in any other form to which any of those shareholders or members have not objected.

   (b) At least 60 days before the first delivery or any delivery to a common address under this subsection, the corporation gives notice to each of the shareholders or members that share that common address that it intends to provide only 1 copy of notices, reports, statements, or other communications to shareholders or members that share a common address.

   (c) The corporation has not received a written objection from any shareholder or member that shares a common address to deliveries under this subsection to that shareholder or member. If it receives a written objection under this subdivision, the corporation within 30 days shall begin providing the objecting shareholder or member with separate copies of any notices, reports, statements, or communications to the shareholders or members, but the corporation may deliver 1 copy of the notices, reports, statements, or communications to all of the shareholders or members at that common address that have not objected.

(4) If a notice or communication is permitted by this act to be transmitted electronically, the notice or communication is given when electronically transmitted to the person entitled to the notice or communication in a manner authorized by the person.

(5) If the administrator is required under this act to give notice to a corporation, the administrator may electronically transmit the notice to the corporation's resident agent in the manner authorized by the corporation.

(6) As used in subsection (3), "address" means a street address, post office box, electronic mail address for electronic transmissions by electronic mail, or telephone facsimile number for electronic transmissions by facsimile.

450.2151 Failure of administrator to file document promptly; notice of failure to file; posting notice on website or sending by mail or electronic mail address; refusal or revocation of authorization of foreign corporation to conduct affairs in state; judicial review.
Sec. 151.

(1) If the administrator fails to promptly file a document, other than an annual report, submitted for filing under this act, the administrator shall within 10 days after receiving a written request to file the document from the person that submitted the document for filing give written notice of the failure to file the document to that person, specifying the reasons for the failure to file the document. The administrator may give written notice under this subsection by posting the notice on the administrator's website; by sending the notice by mail to the address provided by the person that submitted the document; or, if the person that submitted the document has provided the administrator with an electronic mail address, by sending the notice to that electronic mail address. The person may seek judicial review of the refusal to file the document under sections 103, 104, and 106 of the administrative procedures act of 1969, 1969 PA 306, MCL 24.303, 24.304, and 24.306.

(2) If the administrator refuses to authorize or revokes the authorization of a foreign corporation to conduct affairs in this state under this act, the foreign corporation may seek judicial review under sections 103, 104, and 106 of the administrative procedures act of 1969, 1969 PA 306, MCL 24.303, 24.304, and 24.306.

Chapter 2 – Formation

450.2201 Incorporators; signing and filing articles of incorporation.
Sec. 201.

(1) One or more persons may be the incorporators of a corporation by signing in ink and filing articles of incorporation for the corporation.

(2) If there are 3 or more incorporators of a corporation, the incorporators may, by suitable resolution adopted by the incorporators at the organization meeting or by written instrument, designate any 1 among themselves to sign the articles of incorporation for that person and the remainder of the incorporators, in which case a copy of the resolution duly certified by the person who acted as secretary at the organization meeting shall be made a part of and filed with the articles of incorporation.

450.2202 Articles of incorporation; contents.
Sec. 202.

The articles of incorporation shall contain all of the following:

(a) The name of the corporation.

(b) The purposes for which the corporation is formed. It is not sufficient to state substantially that the corporation may engage in any activity within the purposes for which a corporation may be formed under this act. If a corporation proposes to organize and operate a school, college, or other educational institution described in section 170 of 1931 PA 327, MCL 450.170, other than a public school academy as defined in section 5 of the revised school code, 1976 PA 451, MCL 380.5, it shall state its educational purposes in its articles of incorporation and comply with all requirements of sections 170 to 177 of 1931 PA 327, MCL 450.170 to 450.177.

(c) If the corporation is formed on a stock basis, the aggregate number of shares that the corporation has authority to issue.

(d) If the corporation is formed on a stock basis, and if the shares are or are to be divided into classes, the designation of each class, the number of shares in each class, and a statement of the relative rights, preferences, and limitations of the shares of each class, to the extent that the designations, numbers, relative rights, preferences, and limitations have been determined.

(e) If the corporation is formed on a nonstock basis, a description and statement of the value of any assets of the corporation that are classified as real and personal property and the terms of the general scheme of financing the corporation.

(f) If the corporation is formed on a nonstock basis, a statement that the corporation is formed on a membership basis or a statement that the corporation is formed on a directorship basis.

(g) The street address, and the mailing address if different from the street address, of the corporation's initial registered office and the name of the corporation's initial resident agent at that address.

(h)   The names and addresses of all the incorporators.
(i)   The duration of the corporation if other than perpetual.

450.2204 Articles of incorporation; provision pertaining to proposed compromise or arrangement or reorganization between corporation and creditors or shareholders.
Sec. 204.

The articles of incorporation may contain the following provision or the substance thereof: When a compromise or arrangement or a plan of reorganization of this corporation is proposed between this corporation and its creditors or any class of them or between this corporation and its shareholders, members, or any class of them, a court of equity jurisdiction within the state, on application of this corporation or of a creditor, shareholder, or member of the corporation, or an application of a receiver appointed for the corporation, may order a meeting of the creditors or class of creditors or of the shareholders or members or class of shareholders or members to be affected by the proposed compromise or arrangement or reorganization, to be summoned in such manner as the court directs. If a majority in number representing 3/4 in value of the creditors or class of creditors, or of the shareholders or members or class of shareholders or members to be affected by the proposed compromise or arrangement or a reorganization, agree to a compromise or arrangement or a reorganization of this corporation as a consequence of the compromise or arrangement, the compromise or arrangement and the reorganization, if sanctioned by the court to which the application has been made, shall be binding on all the creditors or class of creditors, or on all the shareholders or members or class of shareholders or members and also on this corporation.

450.2205 Articles of incorporation; including provision of MCL 450.2204; effect on creditors, shareholders, or members of corporation; administration and enforcement of provision by circuit court; restraining actions and proceedings against corporation; appointment and powers of temporary receiver.
Sec. 205.

(1)   When the provision of section 204 is included in the original articles of incorporation of a corporation, all persons who become creditors, shareholders, or members of the corporation are deemed to have become creditors, shareholders, or members subject in all respects to that provision, and it shall be binding upon them.
(2)   When that provision is inserted in the articles of a corporation by an amendment of the articles, all persons who become creditors, shareholders, or members of the corporation after the amendment becomes effective are deemed to have become creditors, shareholders, or members subject in all respects to that provision, and it shall be binding upon them.

(3) The circuit court may administer and enforce the provision and restrain, during the process of an action, actions and proceedings against the corporation with respect to which the court so restraining has begun the administration or enforcement of the provision, and appoint a temporary receiver for the corporation and grant the receiver such powers as are deemed proper.

450.2209 Articles of incorporation; additional provisions; liability of director or volunteer officer.
Sec. 209.

(1) The articles of incorporation may contain any provision that is not inconsistent with this act and not expressly prohibited by any other statute of this state, including, but not limited to, any of the following:
   (a) A provision for management of the business and conduct of the affairs of the corporation, or creating, defining, limiting, or regulating the powers of the corporation, its directors, officers, members, or shareholders, or a class of directors, shareholders, or members.
   (b) A provision that under this act is required or permitted to be set forth in the bylaws.
   (c) A provision that eliminates or limits a director's or volunteer officer's liability to the corporation, its shareholders, or its members for money damages for any action taken or any failure to take any action as a director or volunteer officer, except liability for any of the following:
      (i) The amount of a financial benefit received by a director or volunteer officer to which he or she is not entitled.
      (ii) Intentional infliction of harm on the corporation, its shareholders, or members.
      (iii) A violation of section 551.
      (iv) An intentional criminal act.
      (v) A liability imposed under section 497(a).
   (d) For a corporation whose purposes, structures, and activities are exclusively those described in section 501(c)(3) of the internal revenue code of 1986, 26 USC 501, a provision that the corporation assumes all liability to any person other than the corporation, its shareholders, or its members for all acts or omissions of a volunteer director occurring on or after January 1, 1988 incurred in the good faith performance of the volunteer director's duties.
   (e) A provision that the corporation assumes the liability for all acts or omissions of a volunteer director, volunteer officer, or other volunteer occurring on or after the effective date of the provision that grants limited liability if all of the following are met:
      (i) The volunteer was acting or reasonably believed he or she was acting within the scope of his or her authority.
      (ii) The volunteer was acting in good faith.
      (iii) The volunteer's conduct did not amount to gross negligence or willful and wanton misconduct.

(iv) The volunteer's conduct was not an intentional tort.

(v) The volunteer's conduct was not a tort arising out of the ownership, maintenance, or use of a motor vehicle for which tort liability may be imposed under section 3135 of the insurance code of 1956, 1956 PA 218, MCL 500.3135.

(f) A provision that reserves to 1 or more members, shareholders, or other persons all or part of the authority to exercise the corporate powers or to manage the business and affairs of the corporation, including the resolution of any issue about which there exists a deadlock among directors, shareholders, or members. A provision authorized under this subsection that limits the discretion or powers of the board relieves the directors of, and imposes on the person or persons in which the discretion or powers are vested, liability for acts or omissions imposed by law on directors to the extent that the discretion or powers of the directors are limited by the provision. The person or persons in which the discretion or powers are vested are treated as a director or directors for the purposes of any limitation or assumption of liability under this section and, except as otherwise provided in the articles of incorporation or bylaws, have the same rights and obligations with respect to indemnification as a director or directors.

(2) If the articles of incorporation contain a provision that eliminates the liability of a volunteer director or volunteer officer that was filed before the effective date of the amendatory act that added this subsection, that provision is considered to eliminate the liability of a director or volunteer officer under subsection (1)(c).

450.2212 Corporate name.
Sec. 212.

(1) The corporate name of a domestic or foreign corporation formed or existing under or subject to this act shall conform to all of the following:

(a) Shall not contain a word or phrase, or abbreviation or derivative of a word or phrase, that indicates or implies that the corporation is formed for a purpose other than 1 or more of the purposes permitted by its articles of incorporation.

(b) Shall distinguish the corporate name in the records in the office of the administrator from all of the following:

(i) The corporate name of any other domestic corporation or foreign corporation authorized to conduct affairs in this state.

(ii) The corporate name of any domestic business corporation or foreign business corporation authorized to transact business in this state.

(iii) A corporate name currently reserved, registered, or assumed under this act or the business corporation act.

(iv) The name of any domestic limited partnership or foreign limited partnership as filed or registered under the Michigan revised uniform limited partnership act, 1982 PA 213, MCL 449.1101 to

449.2108, or any name currently reserved or assumed under that act.

(v) The name of any domestic limited liability company or foreign limited liability company as filed or registered under the Michigan limited liability company act, 1993 PA 23, MCL 450.4101 to 450.5200, or any name currently reserved or assumed under that act.

(c) Shall not contain a word or phrase, an abbreviation, or derivative of a word or phrase, the use of which is prohibited or restricted by any other statute of this state, unless the use of the name complies with that restriction.

(2) If a foreign corporation is unable to obtain a certificate of authority to conduct affairs in this state because its corporate name does not comply with subsection (1), the foreign corporation may apply for authority to conduct affairs in this state by adding to its corporate name in the application a word, abbreviation, or other distinctive and distinguishing element, or alternatively, adopting for use in this state an assumed name otherwise available for use. If in the judgment of the administrator that name would comply with the provisions of subsection (1), that subsection does not prevent the administrator from issuing the foreign corporation a certificate of authority to conduct affairs in this state. The certificate issued to the foreign corporation shall be issued in the name applied for and the foreign corporation shall use that name in all its dealings with the administrator and in the conduct of its affairs in this state.

(3) A charitable purpose corporation may use the word "foundation" in its corporate name or in an assumed name. This subsection does not prohibit a corporation from continuing to use the word "foundation" in its corporate name or in an assumed name if the corporation was in existence and used the word "foundation" in its corporate name or in an assumed name before the effective date of the amendatory act that added this sentence.

(4) The fact that a corporation complies with this section does not create substantive rights to use of a corporate name.

450.2213 Assuming name that implies corporation is banking corporation, insurance or surety company, or trust company prohibited.
Sec. 213.

A corporation formed or existing under or subject to this act shall not assume a name which implies that it is a banking corporation, an insurance or surety company, or a trust company.

450.2215 Reservation of right to use corporate name; application; duration; expiration; transfer of right to exclusive use of reserved corporate name.
Sec. 215.

(1) A person may reserve the right to use a corporate name by executing and filing an application to reserve the name. If the administrator finds that the name is available for corporate use, he or she shall reserve it for exclusive use of the applicant for a period that expires at the end of the sixth full calendar month following the month in which the application was filed.

(2) A person may transfer a right to exclusive use of a corporate name reserved under subsection (1) to another person by filing a notice of the transfer, executed by the applicant for which the name was reserved, that states the name and address of the transferee.

450.2217 Conduct of affairs under assumed name or names other than corporate name; certificate of assumed name; duration; extensions; notification of impending expiration; enterprises participating together in partnership or joint venture; transfer or use of assumed name in merger or conversion.
Sec. 217.

(1) Except as provided in section 212 or otherwise prohibited by law, a domestic or foreign corporation may conduct its affairs under any assumed name or names other than its corporate name, by filing a certificate stating the true name of the corporation and the assumed name under which its affairs are to be conducted. A certificate of assumed name is effective, unless sooner terminated by filing a certificate of termination or by the dissolution or withdrawal of the corporation, for a period that expires on December 31 of the fifth full calendar year following the year in which it was filed. A certificate of assumed name may be extended for additional consecutive periods of 5 full calendar years each by filing similar certificates not earlier than 90 days preceding the expiration of the initial or a subsequent 5-year period. The administrator shall notify the corporation of the impending expiration of the certificate of assumed name not later than 90 days before the expiration of the initial or subsequent 5-year period. If authorized by the corporation, the administrator may electronically transmit the notice to the resident agent of the corporation. A certificate of assumed name filed under this section does not create substantive rights to the use of a particular assumed name.

(2) Two or more corporations, or 1 or more corporations and 1 or more business corporations, limited partnerships, limited liability companies, or other enterprises that participate together in a partnership or joint venture may assume the same name. Each participant corporation shall file a certificate under this section.

(3) A corporation that participates in a merger, or any other entity that participates in a merger under section 735 or 736a, may transfer to the surviving entity the use of an assumed name for which a certificate of

assumed name is on file with the administrator before the merger, if the transfer is noted in the certificate of merger under section 707(1)(f), 712(1)(c), or 736a(3)(f) or other applicable statute. The use of an assumed name transferred under this subsection may continue for the remaining effective period of the certificate of assumed name on file before the merger, and the surviving entity may terminate or extend the certificate of assumed name under subsection (1).

(4) A corporation that survives a merger may use as an assumed name the corporate name of a merging corporation, or the name of any other entity that participates in the merger under section 735 or 736a, by filing a certificate of assumed name under subsection (1) or by providing for the use of the name as an assumed name in the certificate of merger. The surviving corporation also may file a certificate of assumed name under subsection (1) or provide in the certificate of merger for the use as an assumed name of an assumed name of a merging entity that is not transferred under subsection (3). A provision in the certificate of merger under this subsection is considered a new certificate of assumed name.

(5) A business organization into which a corporation has converted under section 745 may use an assumed name of the converting corporation, if the corporation has a certificate of assumed name for that assumed name on file with the administrator before the conversion, by providing for the use of the name as an assumed name in the certificate of conversion. The use of an assumed name under this subsection may continue for the remaining effective period of the certificate of assumed name on file before the conversion, and the surviving business organization may terminate or extend the certificate of assumed name under subsection (1).

(6) A corporation into which 1 or more business organizations have converted under section 746 may use as an assumed name the name of any business organization converting into that corporation, or use as an assumed name an assumed name of that business organization, by filing a certificate of assumed name under subsection (1) or by providing for the use of that name or assumed name as an assumed name of the corporation in the certificate of conversion. A provision in the certificate of conversion under this subsection is considered a new certificate of assumed name.

450.2221 Corporate existence to begin on effective date of articles of incorporation; filing as conclusive evidence that conditions precedent fulfilled and corporation formed; exception.
Sec. 221.

The corporate existence of a corporation begins on the effective date of the articles of incorporation as provided in section 131. Filing of the articles of incorporation is conclusive evidence that all conditions precedent required to be performed under this act have been fulfilled and that the corporation has been formed under this act, except in an action or special proceeding by the attorney general.

450.2223 Selection of board and adoption of bylaws; first meeting; notice; quorum; transaction of business.
Sec. 223.

Before or after filing of the articles of incorporation a majority of the incorporators at a meeting or by written instrument, shall select a board and may adopt bylaws. On or after the filing date of the articles, any member of the board may call the first meeting of the board upon not less than 3 days' notice by mail to each director. A majority of the directors constitutes a quorum for the first meeting of the board. At the first meeting, the board may adopt bylaws, elect officers, and transact such other business as may come before the meeting.

450.2231 Bylaws; adoption; amendment or repeal; contents.
Sec. 231.

(1) Except if the power to adopt, amend, or repeal the bylaws is reserved exclusively to the corporation's shareholders, its members, or its board in the articles of incorporation:
   (a) The initial bylaws of a corporation shall be adopted by its incorporators, its shareholders, its members, or its board.
   (b) The shareholders, the members, or the board may amend or repeal the bylaws or adopt new bylaws.
   (c) The shareholders or members may prescribe in the bylaws that any bylaw adopted by them shall not be amended or repealed by the board.
(2) The bylaws may contain any provision for the regulation and management of the affairs of the corporation not inconsistent with law or the articles of incorporation.

450.2241 Registered office; resident agent.
Sec. 241.

Each domestic corporation and each foreign corporation authorized to conduct affairs in this state shall have and continuously maintain in this state both of the following:
   (a) A registered office that may be the same as its place of business.
   (b) A resident agent. Any of the following may serve as resident agent:
      (i) An individual resident in this state whose business office or residence is identical with the registered office.
      (ii) A domestic corporation, a domestic business corporation, a foreign corporation, a foreign business corporation, a limited liability company, or another entity, if it is authorized to conduct affairs or transact business in this state and it has a business office identical with the registered office.

450.2242 Change of registered office or resident agent; statement.
Sec. 242.

(1) A domestic corporation or a foreign corporation authorized to conduct affairs in this state may change its registered office or change its resident agent, or both, by filing a statement with the department. The statement may be executed by any of the individuals described in section 132 or by the secretary or assistant secretary of the corporation. The statement shall provide all of the following information:
   (a) The corporate name.
   (b) The street address of the corporation's registered office at the time of filing, and its mailing address if different from its street address.
   (c) If the address of the corporation's registered office is changed, the street address and the mailing address, if different from the street address, to which the registered office is to be changed.
   (d) The name of the corporation's resident agent at the time of filing.
   (e) If the corporation's resident agent is changed, the name of its successor resident agent.
   (f) That the address of the corporation's registered office and the address of its resident agent, as changed, will be identical.
   (g) That the change was authorized by resolution duly adopted by the corporation's board, or, if no board has been appointed, by the incorporators.
(2) If a resident agent changes its business or residence address to another place within this state, the resident agent may change the address of the registered office of any domestic or foreign corporation of which the person is a resident agent by filing the statement required under subsection (1), except that the statement need only be signed by the resident agent, need not be responsive to subsection (1)(e) or (g), and shall recite that a copy of the statement has been mailed to the corporation.

450.2243 Resident agent; resignation; notice; appointment of successor; termination of appointment of resigning resident agent; registered office of corporation.
Sec. 243.

A resident agent of a domestic or foreign corporation may resign by filing a written notice of resignation with the president or a vice president of the corporation and with the administrator. A corporation shall promptly appoint a successor resident agent after its resident agent has resigned. The appointment of a resigning resident agent terminates when a successor is appointed or 30 days after receipt of the notice by the administrator, whichever first occurs. When a resignation becomes effective under this section, the business or residence address of the resigned agent is no longer the registered office of the corporation.

450.2246 Resident agent; service of process, notice, or demand; resident agent as agent of director or officer in certain action; forwarding process to director or officer; electronic transmission of notice.
Sec. 246.

(1) The resident agent appointed by a corporation is an agent of the corporation on which any process, notice, or demand required or permitted by law to be served on the corporation may be served.

(2) If an individual, whether a resident or nonresident of this state, accepts election, appointment, or employment as a director or officer of a corporation formed under this act or in existence on the effective date of this act, the acceptance is considered an appointment of the resident agent of the corporation as his or her agent on which process may be served while he or she is a director or officer, in any action commenced in a court of general jurisdiction in this state, arising out of or founded on any action of the domestic corporation or of the individual as a director or officer of the domestic corporation. After accepting service of process, the resident agent shall promptly forward it to the director or officer at his or her last known address.

(3) The administrator may serve a notice described in subsection (1) by electronically transmitting the notice to the resident agent of the corporation in the manner authorized by the corporation.

450.2251 Corporate purposes; conduct of lawful activities during war or national emergency.
Sec. 251.

(1) A corporation may be formed under this act for any lawful purposes not involving pecuniary gain or profit for its officers, directors, shareholders, or members, other than a purpose for which a corporation may be formed under any other statute of this state and that statute expressly prohibits formation under this act. A corporation that is formed under this act for a purpose for which a corporation may be formed under another statute of this state does not have any powers or privileges conferred by that other statute that are not conferred under this act.

(2) In time of war or other national emergency, a corporation may take any lawful action to provide aid, including any business activity, notwithstanding the purposes set forth in its articles of incorporation, at the request or direction of a competent governmental authority.

450.2261 Corporate powers; inconsistency between certain acts; corporate existence in perpetuity; fixed limitation or term; waiver of right to perpetual existence; nonprofit power corporation; public school academy; providing services in learned profession; personal liability and

accountability for negligent or wrongful acts or misconduct; indemnification.
Sec. 261.

(1) A corporation, subject to any limitation provided in this act, in any other statute of this state, or in its articles of incorporation, has the power in furtherance of its corporate purposes to do any of the following:
   (a) Have perpetual duration.
   (b) Sue and be sued in all courts and participate in actions and proceedings judicial, administrative, arbitrative, or otherwise, in the same manner as an individual.
   (c) Have a corporate seal, alter the seal, and use it by causing it or a facsimile to be affixed, impressed, or reproduced in any other manner.
   (d) Adopt, amend, or repeal bylaws, including emergency bylaws, relating to the purposes of the corporation, the conduct of its affairs, its rights and powers, and the rights and powers of its shareholders, members, directors, or officers.
   (e) Elect or appoint officers, employees, and other agents of the corporation, prescribe their duties, fix their compensation and the compensation of directors, and indemnify corporate directors, officers, employees, and agents.
   (f) Purchase, receive, take by grant, gift, devise, bequest, or otherwise, lease, or otherwise acquire, own, hold, improve, administer, employ, use, and otherwise deal in and with, real or personal property, or an interest in real or personal property, wherever situated, either absolutely, in trust, or as an endowment or donor restricted fund, and without limitation as to amount or value.
   (g) Sell, convey, lease, exchange, transfer, or otherwise dispose of, or mortgage or pledge, or create a security interest in, any of its property, or an interest in the property, wherever situated.
   (h) Purchase, take, receive, subscribe for, or otherwise acquire, own, hold, vote, employ, sell, lend, lease, exchange, transfer, or otherwise dispose of, mortgage, pledge, use, and otherwise deal in and with, bonds and other obligations, shares or other securities or interests or memberships issued by others, whether engaged in similar or different business, governmental, or other activities, including banking corporations or trust companies. A corporation organized or conducting affairs in this state under this act shall not guarantee or become surety on a bond or other undertaking securing the deposit of public money.
   (i) Make contracts, give guarantees, and incur liabilities, borrow money at rates of interest as the corporation may determine, issue its notes, bonds, and other obligations, and secure any of its obligations by mortgage or pledge of any of its property or an interest in the property, wherever situated. Without limiting the preceding, these powers include the powers to give guarantees and to incur joint indebtedness that are necessary or convenient to the conduct, promotion, or attainment of the purposes of any of the following entities, whether or

not subject to this act, and those guarantees or joint indebtedness is considered to be in furtherance of the corporate purpose of the contracting corporation:

   (i) A corporation, foreign corporation, domestic business corporation, or foreign business corporation, if all of its outstanding shares are owned, directly or indirectly, or all of the outstanding memberships are owned or controlled, directly or indirectly, by any of the following:

     (A) The contracting corporation.

     (B) A directorship corporation whose directors are all elected or appointed, directly or indirectly, by the contracting corporation.

     (C) A domestic or foreign limited liability company, if all of its membership interests are owned or controlled, directly or indirectly, by the contracting corporation.

   (ii) A corporation or foreign corporation that owns or controls, directly or indirectly, all of the outstanding shares of the contracting corporation; or that owns or controls, directly or indirectly, all of the outstanding membership interests of the contracting corporation; or that elects or appoints, directly or indirectly, all of the directors of the contracting directorship corporation.

   (iii) A corporation or foreign corporation, if all of its outstanding shares are owned or controlled, directly or indirectly, or all of its outstanding memberships are owned or controlled, directly or indirectly, by an affiliate; or a directorship corporation, if all of its directors are elected or appointed, directly or indirectly, by an affiliate. As used in this subparagraph, "affiliate" means a nonprofit corporation, whether or not subject to this act, or a foreign corporation, that owns or controls, directly or indirectly, all of the outstanding shares of the contracting corporation; or that owns or controls, directly or indirectly, all of the outstanding memberships of the contracting corporation; or that elects or appoints, directly or indirectly, all of the directors of the contracting corporation if it is a directorship corporation.

(j) Lend money, invest and reinvest its funds, and take and hold real and personal property as security for the payment of funds loaned, invested, or reinvested.

(k) Make donations for any of the following: the public welfare; a community fund; or hospital; or a charitable, educational, scientific, civic, or similar purpose. A corporation also has the power to provide aid in time of war or other national emergency.

(l) Pay pensions, establish and carry out pension, federally qualified profit sharing, savings, thrift, and other retirement, incentive, and benefit plans, trusts, and provisions for any of its directors, officers, and employees.

(m) Purchase, receive, take, otherwise acquire, own, hold, sell, lend, exchange, transfer, otherwise dispose of, pledge, use, and otherwise deal in and with its own shares, bonds, and other securities.

(n) Participate with others in any domestic corporation, foreign corporation, domestic business corporation, foreign business corporation, partnership, limited partnership, limited liability company, limited liability partnership, joint venture, or other association of any kind, or in any transaction, undertaking, or agreement that the participating corporation would have power to conduct by itself, whether or not the participation involves sharing or delegation of control with or to others.

(o) Cease its corporate activities and dissolve.

(p) Conduct its affairs, carry on its operations, and have offices and exercise the powers granted under this act in any jurisdiction in or outside the United States, and, in the case of a corporation the purpose or purposes of which require the transaction of business, the receipt and payment of money, the care and custody of property, and other incidental business matters, transact that business, receive, collect, and disburse that money, and engage in those other incidental business matters as are naturally or properly within the scope of its articles.

(q) Have and exercise all powers necessary or convenient to effect any purpose for which the corporation is formed.

(2) A corporation that is subject to the uniform prudent management of institutional funds act, 2009 PA 87, MCL 451.921 to 451.931, has all powers granted under both this act and that act. However, in the event of an inconsistency between the 2 acts, the uniform prudent management of institutional funds act, 2009 PA 87, MCL 451.921 to 451.931, controls.

(3) The corporate existence of all corporations incorporated before January 1, 1983, without capital stock, for religious, benevolent, social, or fraternal purposes, shall be considered to be in perpetuity. A limitation or term fixed in the articles or in the law under which the corporation originally incorporated is not effective unless the corporation affirmatively waived its right to perpetual existence after September 18, 1931, by fixing a definite term of existence by amendment to its articles.

(4) Any nonprofit power corporation that is authorized to furnish electric service may construct, maintain, and operate its lines along, over, across, or under any public places, streets, and highways, and across or under the waters in this state, with all necessary erections and fixtures. A nonprofit power corporation may exercise the power of eminent domain, in the manner provided by the uniform condemnation procedures act, 1980 PA 87, MCL 213.51 to 213.75. As a condition to the exercise of any of these powers, nonprofit corporations are subject to the jurisdiction of the Michigan public service commission under 1909 PA 106, MCL 460.551 to 460.559, 1919 PA 419, MCL 460.54 to 460.62, and 1939 PA 3, MCL 460.1 to 460.11.

(5) A corporation formed under this act that is operating a public school academy as defined in section 5 of the revised school code, 1976 PA 451,

MCL 380.5, is a public body corporate and a governmental agency and shall have all powers granted under this act and under the revised school code, 1976 PA 451, MCL 380.1 to 380.1853. However, in the event of an inconsistency between this act and the revised school code, the revised school code shall control.

(6) Subject to the limitations on the practice of law by corporations contained in 1917 PA 354, MCL 450.681, a domestic corporation may be formed and a foreign corporation may be authorized to conduct affairs in this state for the purpose of providing services in a learned profession and may employ and enter into other arrangements with duly licensed or authorized individuals who shall furnish those services on behalf of the corporation.

(7) Except as provided in section 209(1)(d) or section 209(1)(e), any duly licensed or authorized individual who is employed by a corporation described in subsection (6) is personally and fully liable and accountable for any negligent or wrongful acts or misconduct committed by him or her, or by any individual under his or her direct supervision and control, while rendering professional services on behalf of the corporation to the person for whom those professional services were being rendered. However, the corporation that employs that duly licensed or authorized individual may indemnify him or her for any resulting liabilities and expenses as provided in this act and under other applicable law.

450.2262 Existing incorporated association or society operating as corporation subject to act; payment of death or sick benefits; reserves; rules; investment of funds securing reserves; statement required of evidence of obligation to pay death and sick benefits.
Sec. 262.

(1) An association or society, not otherwise provided for here or by other statute, incorporated before January 1, 1983, and now existing, whose purpose is to provide for the relief of distressed members, visitation of the sick, and the payment of a voluntary sick benefit to or for members not exceeding $2,000.00 on account of any 1 member, or the buying and selling of products for its members without direct pecuniary profit to the association or its members may operate as a corporation subject to this act. The ladies Lutheran benevolent federation of Michigan, now incorporated as a nonprofit corporation, may pay death benefits in an amount not exceeding $500.00 to any 1 person. The metropolitan club of America, inc., national spirit, and the ladies auxiliary of the metropolitan clubs of America, national spirit, which are incorporated as nonprofit corporations, may pay death benefits in an amount not to exceed $1,000.00 to any 1 person. The Venetian club of mutual aid, incorporated as a nonprofit corporation, may pay death and sick benefits in an amount not to exceed $10,000.00 to any 1 person. The Warren firemen's benevolent association may pay death and sick benefits in an amount not to exceed $20,000.00 to any 1 person. The Lansing firemen's benefit association may pay death and sick benefits in an amount not to exceed $2,000.00 to any 1 person. The

Sanilac county police and firemen's fund may pay death and sick benefits in an amount not to exceed $3,000.00 to any 1 person. The Italian-American brotherhood society may pay death and sick benefits in an amount not to exceed $3,000.00 to any 1 person. The Italian-American fraternal club of Dearborn may pay death and sick benefits in an amount not to exceed $500.00 to any 1 person. The Michigan licensed beverage association may pay death and sick benefits in an amount not to exceed $5,000.00 to any 1 person who is a licensee of the Michigan liquor control commission. The Westland fire fighters' benevolent association may pay death and sick benefits in an amount not to exceed $7,500.00 to any 1 person. The Livonia benevolent association for fire fighters and police officers may pay death and sick benefits in an amount not to exceed $5,000.00 to any 1 person. The Midland fire fighters' benefit fund may pay death and sick benefits in an amount not to exceed $10,000.00 to any 1 person. The incorporated branches of the fraternal order of eagles within this state may pay death benefits of $350.00 or sickness benefits of $350.00, but not a combination of death and sickness benefits that would exceed $500.00 to any 1 person.

(2) The entities specified in this section and organized before January 1, 1983, and providing for the payment of death or sick benefits under this section in an amount exceeding $1,000.00 to 1 person shall by January 1, 1980, establish and maintain reserves in an amount estimated in the aggregate to provide for the payment of all losses and claims incurred, whether reported or unreported, which are unpaid and for which the entity may be liable and to provide for the expense of adjustment or settlement of losses and claims. The reserves shall be computed in accordance with rules promulgated by the commissioner of insurance, after due notice and hearing, upon reasonable consideration of the ascertained experiences and the character of such kinds of business for the purpose of adequately protecting the members and securing the solvency of the corporations. The funds of the entities securing the reserves shall be invested only in securities permitted by the laws of this state for the investment of assets of life insurance companies.

(3) An entity specified in this section that obligates itself to the payment of death and sick benefits to its members shall not make, issue, or deliver in this state a certificate or other written evidence of the obligation unless the certificate or other written evidence has conspicuously printed on the first page in boldface type not smaller than 10 point the following statement: This organization does not operate under the supervision of the Michigan insurance bureau.

450.2271 Act of corporation and transfer of property to or by corporation not invalid where corporation without capacity or power; assertion of lack of capacity or power.
Sec. 271.

An act of a corporation and a transfer of real or personal property to or by a corporation, otherwise lawful, is not invalid because the corporation was without capacity or power to do the act or make or receive the transfer of property. However the lack of capacity or power may be asserted:

(a) By a shareholder or member, or by a director who has not authorized or consented to the act or transfer, in an action against the corporation to enjoin the doing of an act or the transfer of real or personal property by or to the corporation.

(b) In an action by or in the right of the corporation to procure a judgment in its favor against an incumbent or former officer or director of the corporation for loss or damage due to an unauthorized act by that person.

(c) In an action or special proceeding by the attorney general to dissolve the corporation or to enjoin it from the conducting of unauthorized affairs.

450.2275 Agreement to pay rate of interest in excess of legal rate; defense of usury prohibited.
Sec. 275.

A domestic corporation or foreign corporation, whether or not formed at the request of a lender or in furtherance of a business enterprise, may by agreement in writing, and not otherwise, agree to pay a rate of interest in excess of the legal rate and is prohibited from asserting the defense of usury in an action on the debt.

Chapter 3 – Structure

450.2301 Payment or distribution of assets, income, or profit; conferring benefits on shareholders or members; transfer of money or property to or for benefit of directors or officers; dividends or distributions to shareholders or members; corporation charging fees or prices for services or products; use, conveyance, or distribution of assets held by corporation for noncharitable purposes; prohibition.
Sec. 301.

(1) A payment or distribution of any part of the assets, income, or profit of a corporation shall conform to the purposes of the corporation.

(2) A corporation may confer benefits on its shareholders or members that conform to the purposes of the corporation.

(3) A corporation shall not make a direct or indirect transfer of money or other property or incur indebtedness to or for the benefit of its directors or officers without adequate consideration. This subsection does not prevent a corporation from paying compensation to its directors and officers in reasonable amounts for services rendered to the corporation or from entering into transactions with officers and directors under sections 545a and 548.

(4) A corporation shall not pay dividends or make distributions of any part of its assets, income, or profit to its shareholders or members, except as follows:

(a) A corporation may pay compensation in reasonable amounts to shareholders or members for services rendered to the corporation.

(b) If a corporation dissolves, the corporation may make distributions of assets, other than assets held for charitable purposes, to shareholders or members as permitted under this act and the corporation may distribute assets held for charitable purposes to 1 or more member or shareholder domestic corporations, foreign corporations, trusts, or similar entities that are organized and operated exclusively for charitable purposes that are not inconsistent with the charitable purposes for which the corporation holds the assets.

(c) The articles of incorporation or bylaws of a corporation whose lawful purposes include providing a benefit to its member or shareholder corporation may provide that the corporation may pay dividends or distribute its income or profit to its member or shareholder corporation.

(d) A corporation whose lawful purposes include selling services or products to its shareholders or members may make distributions of profit to its shareholders or members if both of the following are met:

(i) The profit is derived solely from the charging of fees or prices to its shareholders or members for its services or products.

(ii) The profit is distributed to the shareholders or members on the basis of, or in proportion to, the fees or prices paid by the shareholders or members to the corporation for its services or products.

(e) A corporation may make distributions to shareholders or members that are domestic or foreign corporations, trusts, or similar nonprofit entities organized and operated exclusively for charitable purposes that are not inconsistent with the purposes of the corporation.

(f) A corporation may make distributions to shareholders or members that are domestic corporations or foreign corporations, trusts, or similar nonprofit entities organized and operated exclusively for purposes that are consistent with the purposes of the corporation.

(g) A corporation may make distributions of stock or memberships in another domestic or foreign corporation to its shareholders or members if its shareholders or members will have no greater rights to receive distributions from the domestic corporation or foreign corporation whose stock or memberships are being distributed than the shareholders or members have with respect to the corporation making the distribution.

(5) A corporation whose lawful activities include the charging of fees or prices for its services or products may receive the income and may make a profit as a result of its receipt. Except as authorized in subsections (2), (3), and (4), the corporation shall apply all of that resulting profit to the maintenance, expansion, or operation of the lawful activities of the corporation.

(6) This act shall not be interpreted in a way that permits assets held by a corporation for charitable purposes to be used, conveyed, or distributed for noncharitable purposes.

450.2302 Corporation organized upon nonstock basis.
Sec. 302.

A corporation shall be organized upon a stock or nonstock basis. A corporation organized upon a nonstock basis shall be organized upon a membership basis or a directorship basis.

450.2303 Corporation organized on stock basis; issuance of shares authorized in articles of incorporation; rules of qualification and government of shareholders.
Sec. 303.

(1) A corporation that is organized on a stock basis may issue the number of shares authorized in its articles of incorporation. All of the following apply to shares issued by the corporation:
   (a) The shares may be all of 1 class or may be divided into 2 or more classes. Each class shall consist of shares that have the designations and relative voting, distribution, liquidation, and other rights, preferences, and limitations, that are consistent with this act, stated in the articles of incorporation or bylaws.
   (b) The articles of incorporation or bylaws may deny, limit, or otherwise prescribe the distribution or liquidation rights of shares of any class. Approval by the shareholders and each affected class of shareholders, if any, voting as a class, is required to adopt, amend, or repeal any bylaw denying, limiting, or otherwise prescribing the voting rights of shareholders or the affected class of shareholders.
   (c) If the shares are divided into 2 or more classes, the shares of each class shall be designated to distinguish them from the shares of the other classes.
   (d) Each share is equal to every other share of the same class.
   (e) Except as otherwise provided by the articles or bylaws, shares of stock are not transferable and shall be canceled upon the death or resignation of the owner of the shares.
   (f) Any of the voting, distribution, liquidation, or other rights, preferences, or limitations of a class may be made dependent on facts or events ascertainable outside of the articles of incorporation or the bylaws, if the manner in which the facts or events operate on the rights, preferences, or limitations is set forth in the articles of incorporation or the bylaws.
(2) A corporation may adopt rules of qualification and government of its shareholders pursuant to its articles and bylaws. Adopted rules shall be reasonable, germane to the purposes of the corporation, and equally

enforced as to all shareholders of the same class. A corporation may provide for the cancellation of the stock of a shareholder that fails to comply with adopted rules without liability for an accounting.

450.2303a Corporation board organized on stock basis; amendment of articles of incorporation deleting reference to par value.
Sec. 303a.

The board of a corporation that is organized on a stock basis by resolution may adopt and file an amendment of the articles of incorporation deleting any reference to par value.

450.2303b Conversion of shares into shares of any class or bonds; conversion of bonds into other bonds or shares; authorization of board to increase authorized shares.
Sec. 303b.

(1) If provided in the articles of incorporation, and subject to the restrictions in sections 301 and 303c, a corporation may issue shares that are convertible at the option of the holder or the corporation or on the happening of a specified event, into shares of any class or into bonds. A corporation may convert shares into bonds only if the corporation could at the time of conversion have purchased, redeemed, or otherwise acquired the shares by issuing the bonds under section 345. Authorized shares, whether issued or unissued, may be made convertible as provided in this subsection within the period and on the terms and conditions authorized in the articles of incorporation.

(2) Unless otherwise provided in the articles of incorporation, and subject to sections 301 and 303c, a corporation may issue bonds that are convertible at the option of the holder into other bonds or into shares of the corporation within the period and on the terms and conditions as fixed by the board.

(3) If the shareholders approve the issue of bonds or shares convertible into shares of the corporation, the approval may provide that the board is authorized by amendment of the articles of incorporation to increase the authorized shares of any class to the number that will be sufficient, when added to the previously authorized but unissued shares of the class, to satisfy the conversion privileges of any bonds or shares convertible into shares of the class.

450.2303c Issuance of bonds convertible into shares or shares convertible into other shares of corporation; condition; cancellation of converted bonds; restoration of converted shares.
Sec. 303c.

(1) A corporation shall not issue bonds that are convertible into shares or shares convertible into other shares of a corporation unless 1 of the following conditions is satisfied:
   (a) A sufficient number of authorized but unissued shares of the appropriate class are reserved by the board to be issued only in satisfaction of the conversion privileges of the convertible bonds or shares when issued.
   (b) The aggregate conversion privileges of the convertible bonds or shares when issued do not exceed the aggregate of any shares reserved under subdivision (a) and any additional shares which the board may authorize under section 303b(3).
(2) The corporation shall cancel bonds that are converted into shares. Unless otherwise provided in the articles of incorporation, shares that are converted into other shares shall be restored to the status of authorized but unissued shares.

450.2303d Shares redeemable in cash, bonds, securities, or other property; prices and conditions.
Sec. 303d.

The articles of incorporation may provide for 1 or more classes of shares that are redeemable, in whole or in part, at the option of the shareholder, or the corporation, or if a specified event occurs. Subject to restrictions imposed in sections 301 and 345, the shares may be redeemable in cash, bonds, securities, or other property at prices, within the periods, and under conditions stated in the articles of incorporation.

450.2304 Corporation organized on membership basis; provisions of articles or bylaws; rights, preferences, and limitations of or on members; classes of members; voting rights; condominium association; homeowners or property owners association; transferability and termination of membership; rules of qualification and government; limitations on membership.
Sec. 304.

(1) Except as otherwise provided in this act, the articles of incorporation or bylaws of a corporation organized on a membership basis may prescribe the number, voting rights, qualifications, liquidation rights, preferences, and limitations, and other rights, preferences, and limitations of or on the members of the corporation.

(2) A corporation organized on a membership basis may have 1 or more classes of members. Except as otherwise provided in this act, any provision for classes of members and the relative number, voting rights, qualifications, liquidation rights, preferences, and limitations, and other rights, preferences, and limitations of or on each class shall be set forth in the articles of incorporation or the bylaws. Each member of any class of members has equal rights with all members of that class.

(3) Except as provided in the articles of incorporation or bylaws, each member of a corporation, regardless of class, is entitled to 1 vote on each matter submitted to a vote of members, unless the articles of incorporation or bylaws deny, limit, or otherwise prescribe the voting rights of any class of members. The members and each affected class of members of a corporation organized on a membership basis, if any, shall adopt, amend, or repeal any bylaw denying, limiting, or otherwise prescribing the voting rights of any class of members.

(4) Members of a condominium association organized for the purposes of administering the affairs of a condominium project are entitled to the voting rights designated in the master deed of the condominium.

(5) The articles of incorporation or the bylaws may provide that members of a homeowners or property owners association are entitled to voting rights based on the number of lots owned by each member.

(6) Except as otherwise provided in this act, the articles of incorporation, or the bylaws, membership is not transferable and is terminated by death, resignation, expulsion, or expiration of a term of membership.

(7) A corporation may adopt rules of qualification and government of its members, including rules of admission to, retention of, and expulsion from membership, under its articles of incorporation or bylaws, if those rules are reasonable, germane to the purposes of the corporation, and equally enforced as to all members.

(8) The articles of incorporation of a corporation that is organized on a membership basis may provide that membership is limited to persons that are members in good standing in other corporations. The articles of incorporation may provide that failure to remain a member in good standing in the other corporation constitutes grounds for expulsion of a member if the articles of incorporation or bylaws of the corporation describe the nature of the evidence that is required and establish the procedures for expulsion of a member.

450.2305 Corporation organized on directorship basis; members; voting; matters subject to action by board of directors.
Sec. 305.

(1) A corporation that is organized on a directorship basis may or may not have members. If a corporation that is organized on a directorship basis has members, the members are not entitled to notice of or to vote on any matter, including, but not limited to, any action denying, limiting, or otherwise prescribing their rights as members or excluding them from membership.

(2) Except as otherwise provided in this act, all matters that are subject to membership vote or other action under this act in the case of a membership corporation are subject to duly authorized action by the board of directors of a directorship corporation. This subsection does not, however, allow the board of directors of a directorship corporation to adopt an amendment to the articles of incorporation under section 407(1) permitting action by the board of directors by less than unanimous written consent.

450.2307 Subscription for shares or membership; enforceability; irrevocability; acceptance; consent to revocation; subscription agreement.
Sec. 307.

(1) A subscription for shares or membership made before or after a corporation is formed is not enforceable unless it is in writing and signed by the subscriber.
(2) A subscription for shares of or membership in a corporation to be formed is irrevocable and the corporation may accept it for a period of 6 months, unless otherwise provided in the subscription agreement or unless all of the subscribers consent to its revocation.
(3) A contract with a corporation to purchase its shares to be issued is a subscription agreement and not an executory contract to purchase shares, unless otherwise provided in the contract.

450.2308 Subscription for shares or membership; payment; installments; call for payment ratable; retention of security interest as security for performance by subscriber.
Sec. 308.

Unless otherwise provided in the subscription agreement:
(a) A subscription for shares or for membership made before or after formation of a corporation shall be paid in full at the time, or in installments and at the times, as the board determines.
(b) A call made by the board for payment on subscriptions is ratable as to all shares or members of the same class.
(c) A corporation may retain a security interest in any shares or memberships as security for performance by the subscriber of the subscriber's obligations under a subscription agreement and subject to the power of sale or rescission on default provided in section 309.

450.2309 Default in payment of amount due under subscription agreement; rights and duties of corporation; limiting and adding to rights and remedies of corporation.
Sec. 309.

(1) If a subscriber defaults in payment of an installment or call or other amount due under a subscription agreement, including an amount that becomes due as a result of a default in performance of any provision of a subscription agreement, the corporation has the following rights and duties:

    (a) It may collect the amount due in the same manner as any other debt owing to it. If the corporation is organized on a stock basis and if the articles of incorporation or bylaws of a corporation permit the transfer of shares, the corporation may at any time before full satisfaction of the claim or a judgment sell the shares in any reasonable manner that is consistent with the articles of incorporation and bylaws. The corporation shall give notice of the time and place of a public sale or of the time after which a private sale may occur, and a written statement of the amount due on each share, to the subscriber personally or by registered or certified mail at least 20 days before the time stated in the notice. The corporation shall pay any excess of net proceeds realized over the amount due plus interest to the subscriber. If the sale is made in good faith, in a reasonable manner and after the notice required in this subdivision, the corporation may recover the difference between the amount due plus interest and the net proceeds of the sale. A good faith purchaser for value acquires title to the sold shares free of any right of the subscriber even if the corporation fails to comply with 1 or more of the requirements of this subdivision.

    (b) It may rescind the subscription, with the effect provided in section 310, and may recover damages for breach of contract. In the case of transferable shares of a corporation organized on a stock basis, unless special circumstances show proximate damages of a different amount, the measure of damages is the difference between the fair market value at the time and place of tender of the shares and the unpaid contract price. A subscription agreement may also provide for liquidated damages in any reasonable amount. The subscriber may have restitution of the amount by which the sum of payments exceeds the corporation's damages for breach of contract, whether fixed by agreement or judgment.

(2) The rights and duties set forth in this section are cumulative so far as is consistent with entitling the corporation to a full and single recovery of the amount due or its damages. A subscription agreement may limit the rights and remedies of the corporation set forth in this section, and may add to them so far as is consistent with this subsection.

450.2310 Rescission of subscription under which part of shares issued and in which security interest retained as cancellation of shares.
Sec. 310.

Rescission by a corporation of a subscription under which a part of the shares subscribed for have been issued and in which the corporation retains a security interest, as provided in section 308(c), effects the cancellation of such shares.

450.2311 Fees or dues required as condition of shareholding or membership; fixing; enforcement.
Sec. 311.

A corporation may fix in the bylaws, or the bylaws may authorize the board to fix, an amount as fees or dues which shareholders or members may be required to pay initially or periodically as a condition of shareholding or admission or retention of membership. The corporation may make bylaws necessary to enforce this requirement, including provisions for cancellation of shares or termination of membership for nonpayment of dues or obligations and for reissuance of shares or reinstatement of membership.

450.2313 Corporation, foreign corporation, business corporation, foreign business corporation, limited liability company, unincorporated association, partnership, or other person as shareholder or member; officers and directors as director of corporation; rights, powers, privileges, and liabilities of shareholders or members.
Sec. 313.

(1) Except as otherwise provided in the articles of incorporation or the bylaws, corporations, foreign corporations, business corporations, foreign business corporations, limited liability companies, unincorporated associations, and partnerships, and any other person without limitation, may be a shareholder or a member of a corporation.

(2) If a corporation, foreign corporation, business corporation, or foreign business corporation is a shareholder or a member in a corporation, its officers or directors may serve as a director of the corporation of which it is a shareholder or member. A corporation, foreign corporation, business corporation, foreign business corporation, limited liability company, unincorporated association, partnership, or other person that is a shareholder or member of a corporation possesses and may exercise all the rights, powers, privileges, and liabilities of individual shareholders or members.

450.2314 Corporation organized on stock basis; issuance of shares; powers.
Sec. 314.

(1) All of the following apply to the issuance of shares by a corporation that is organized on a stock basis:
    (a) The board may authorize shares that are issued for no consideration or for consideration that may consist of any tangible or intangible property or benefit to the corporation, including, but not limited to, cash, promissory notes, services performed, contracts for services to be performed, or other securities of the corporation.
    (b) A determination by the board that any consideration received or to be received for issued shares is conclusive concerning the nature and amount of consideration for the issuance of shares in determining whether the shares are validly issued, fully paid, and nonassessable.
    (c) When the corporation receives the consideration for which the board authorized the issuance of shares, the shares issued are fully paid and nonassessable and the subscriber has all the rights and privileges of a holder of the shares.
(2) The powers granted in this section to the board may be reserved to the shareholders in the articles of incorporation.

450.2317 Person purchasing shares of corporation; person holding stock or membership in fiduciary or representative capacity; person becoming assignee, transferee, or pledgee of shares or membership; liability.
Sec. 317.

(1) A person that purchases shares of a corporation from the corporation or purchases a membership in a corporation is not liable to the corporation or its creditors with respect to the shares or membership except to pay the consideration for the issuance of the shares or membership.
(2) A person that holds stock or membership in a corporation in a fiduciary or representative capacity is not personally liable to the corporation as the holder of or subscriber for shares or membership, but the estate or funds for which the person is holding the stock or membership are liable to the corporation as the holder or subscriber.
(3) A person that becomes an assignee, transferee, or pledgee of shares or membership or of a subscription for shares or membership in good faith and without knowledge or notice that the full consideration has not been paid is not liable to the corporation or its creditors for any unpaid portion of the consideration, but the original holder or subscriber and any assignee or transferee before an assignment or transfer to a person that takes in good faith and without knowledge or notice remains liable for that amount.
(4) Unless otherwise provided in the articles of incorporation, a person that is a shareholder or member of a corporation is not personally liable for the acts or debts of the corporation except that the person may become personally liable by reason of the person's own acts or conduct.

450.2327 Charges and expenses of organization or reorganization; sale or underwriting expenses and compensation; payment or allowance.
Sec. 327.

The reasonable charges and expenses of organization or reorganization of a corporation, and the reasonable expenses of and compensation for the sale or underwriting of its shares, may be paid or allowed by the corporation out of the consideration received by it in payment for its shares without thereby rendering the shares not fully paid or assessable.

450.2331 Representation of shares by certificates; signatures of officers; seal; facsimiles.
Sec. 331.

Except as provided in section 336, the shares of a corporation shall be represented by certificates that are signed by the chairperson of the board, vice-chairperson of the board, president or a vice-president and that also may be signed by another officer of the corporation. The corporation may seal the certificate with the seal of the corporation or a facsimile of the seal. The signatures of the officers may be facsimiles. If an officer who has signed or whose facsimile signature has been placed on a certificate ceases to be an officer before the certificate is issued, the corporation may issue the certificate and his or her signature has the same effect as if he or she were an officer on the date of issue.

450.2332 Certificate representing shares; required statements.
Sec. 332.

(1) A certificate that represents shares issued by a corporation shall state on its face all of the following:
    (a) That the corporation is a nonprofit corporation formed under the laws of this state.
    (b) The name of the person to which the certificate is issued.
    (c) The number and class of shares that the certificate represents.
    (d) A statement that the shares are not transferable, unless the articles or bylaws provide that shares are transferable. If the shares are transferable, the certificate shall state any conditions or limitations on transferability of the shares.
    (e) The act under which the corporation was formed.
(2) A certificate that represents shares issued by a corporation that is authorized to issue shares of more than 1 class shall set forth on its face or back or state on its face or back that the corporation will furnish to a shareholder, on request and without charge, a full statement of the designation, relative rights, preferences, and limitations of the shares of each class the corporation is authorized to issue.

450.2334 Lost or destroyed certificate; issuance of new certificate; bond.
Sec. 334.

A corporation may issue a new certificate for shares or fractional shares in place of a certificate theretofore issued by it, alleged to have been lost or destroyed, and the board may require the owner of the lost or destroyed certificate, or the owner's legal representative, to give the corporation a bond sufficient to indemnify the corporation against any claim that may be made against it on account of the alleged lost or destroyed certificate or the issuance of such a new certificate.

450.2336 Authorization of shares without certificates.
Sec. 336.

(1) Unless the articles of incorporation or bylaws provide otherwise, the board of a corporation may authorize the issuance of some or all of the shares of any or all of its classes of shares without certificates. The authorization does not affect shares that are already represented by certificates until they are surrendered to the corporation.
(2) Within a reasonable time after the issuance or transfer of shares without certificates under this section, the corporation shall send the shareholder a written statement of the information required on certificates under section 332 and, if applicable, sections 472 and 488.

450.2338 Issuing fractions of shares; powers of corporation; providing opportunity to purchase additional fractions of share or scrip.
Sec. 338.

(1) A corporation may issue fractions of a share and may do any 1 or more of the following:
   (a) Issue certificates for fractions of shares that entitle the holders to exercise voting rights and receive distributions permitted under section 301 in proportion to their fractional holdings.
   (b) Pay in cash the fair value of fractions of shares as of the time when those entitled to receive the fractions are determined.
   (c) Issue scrip in registered or bearer form over the manual or facsimile signature of an officer of the corporation or of its agent, exchangeable as provided in the scrip for full shares. The scrip does not entitle the holder to any right of a shareholder except as provided in the scrip. A corporation shall issue scrip subject to the condition that it becomes void if it is not exchanged for certificates that represent full shares before a specified date. The scrip may be subject to the condition that the shares for which the scrip is exchangeable may be sold by the corporation and the proceeds of the sale distributed to the holders of the scrip, or subject to any other condition that is established by the board.

(2) A corporation may provide reasonable opportunity for a person that is entitled to fractions of a share or scrip to sell them or to purchase additional fractions of a share or scrip that the person needs to acquire a full share.

450.2341a Issuance of shares pro rata and without consideration; issuance of shares as share dividend; "share dividend" defined.
Sec. 341a.

(1) Unless the articles of incorporation provide otherwise, a corporation may issue shares pro rata and without consideration to the corporation's shareholders or to the shareholders of 1 or more classes as a share dividend.
(2) A corporation may not issue shares of 1 class as a share dividend in respect of shares of another class unless the articles authorize the issuance, the issuance is consistent with the limitations in section 301, and either a majority of the votes entitled to be cast by the class to be issued approve the issue or there are no outstanding shares of the class to be issued.
(3) As used in this section, "share dividend" means shares issued under subsection (1).

450.2343 Preemptive right of shareholder of corporation organized on stock basis to acquire unissued shares; extent; statement; principles; "shares" defined.
Sec. 343.

(1) The shareholders of a corporation organized on a stock basis do not have a preemptive right to acquire the corporation's unissued shares except to the extent provided in the articles of incorporation or by agreement between the corporation and 1 or more shareholders.
(2) If a statement is included in the articles of incorporation or an agreement described in subsection (1) that the corporation elects to have preemptive rights, or words of similar import are included in the articles or agreement, the following principles apply except to the extent the articles of incorporation or agreement expressly provide otherwise:
   (a) The shareholders of the corporation have a preemptive right, granted on uniform terms and conditions prescribed by the board, to provide a fair and reasonable opportunity to exercise the right to acquire proportional amounts of the corporation's unissued shares if the board decides to issue them.
   (b) A shareholder may waive his or her preemptive right. A waiver evidenced by a writing is irrevocable even though it is not supported by consideration.
   (c) There is no preemptive right with respect to any of the following:
      (i) Shares that are authorized in the articles of incorporation and are issued within 6 months after the effective date of incorporation.
      (ii) Shares that are not issued for money.

(d) Holders of shares of any class that do not have general voting rights but do have preferential rights to distributions or assets do not have preemptive rights with respect to shares of any class.

(e) Holders of shares of any class that have general voting rights but do not have preferential rights to distributions or assets do not have preemptive rights with respect to shares of any class with preferential rights to distributions or assets unless the shares with preferential rights are convertible into or carry a right to subscribe for or acquire shares without preferential rights.

(f) Shares that are subject to preemptive rights that are not acquired by shareholders may be issued to any person for a period of 1 year after the shares are offered to shareholders at a consideration set by the board that is not lower than the consideration set for the exercise of preemptive rights. An offer at a lower consideration or after the expiration of 1 year is subject to the shareholders' preemptive rights.

(3) The preemptive rights, if any, whether created by statute or common law, of shareholders of a corporation formed before January 1, 1973, are not affected by subsections (1) and (2). A corporation may alter or abolish its shareholders' preemptive rights by an amendment to its articles of incorporation.

(4) As used in this section, "shares" includes a security convertible into or carrying a right to subscribe for or acquire shares.

450.2344 Acquisition of own shares or memberships; amendment of articles of incorporation.
Sec. 344.

(1) Subject to restrictions imposed under this act or the articles of incorporation, a corporation that is organized on a stock or membership basis may acquire its own shares or memberships. Except as provided in subsection (4), those shares or memberships constitute authorized but unissued shares or memberships.

(2) If the articles of incorporation prohibit reissue of any shares or memberships acquired under subsection (1), the board by resolution shall adopt and file any necessary amendment to the articles of incorporation to reduce the number of authorized shares or memberships accordingly.

(3) A corporation shall not acquire its own shares or memberships by purchase, redemption, or otherwise unless after the acquisition there remain outstanding shares or memberships that possess, collectively, voting rights or unless the articles of incorporation have been amended to provide that the corporation is organized on a directorship basis after the acquisition.

(4) A corporation that acquires its own shares or memberships may grant a security interest in the shares or memberships as security for the payment of the purchase price of the shares or memberships. Any shares or memberships acquired by the corporation in which it has granted a security interest are not canceled and do not constitute authorized but unissued shares or memberships until the corporation pays the purchase price. If a

corporation has granted a security interest in its own shares or memberships, the shares or memberships shall not be voted directly or indirectly and are not counted in determining the total number of issued shares or members entitled to vote at any given time, except to the extent provided by the agreement creating the security interest in the event of default. When the purchase price is paid, the shares or memberships are canceled and constitute authorized but unissued shares or memberships. If the articles of incorporation prohibit reissue of canceled shares or memberships, then the board by resolution shall adopt and file any amendment to the articles of incorporation required under subsection (2).

450.2345 Distributions to shareholders or members.
Sec. 345.

(1) A board may authorize and the corporation may make distributions to its shareholders or members that are permitted in section 301, subject to subsection (3) and any restriction in the articles of incorporation.
(2) If the board does not fix the record date for determining shareholders or members entitled to a distribution, other than a distribution involving a purchase, redemption, or acquisition of the corporation's shares or memberships, the record date is the date the board authorizes the distribution.
(3) A corporation shall not make a distribution if after giving it effect the corporation would not be able to pay its debts as the debts become due in the usual course of business, or the corporation's total assets would be less than the sum of its total liabilities plus, unless the articles of incorporation permit otherwise, the amount that would be needed, if the corporation were dissolved at the time of the distribution, to satisfy the preferential rights on dissolution of shareholders or members whose preferential rights are superior to those that receive the distribution.
(4) The board may base a determination that a distribution is not prohibited under subsection (3) on financial statements prepared on the basis of accounting practices and principles that are reasonable in the circumstances, on a fair valuation, or on any other method that is reasonable.
(5) The effect of a distribution under subsection (3) is measured at the following times:
  (a) Except as provided in subsection (7), for distributions by purchase, redemption, or other acquisition of the corporation's shares or memberships, as of the earlier of the date money or other property is transferred or debt incurred by the corporation, or the date the shareholder or member ceases to be a shareholder or member with respect to the acquired shares or ceases to be a member.
  (b) For any other distribution of indebtedness, as of the date the indebtedness is authorized if distribution occurs within 120 days after the date of authorization or the date the indebtedness is distributed if it occurs more than 120 days after the date of authorization.

(c) For any other purpose, as of the date the distribution is authorized if the payment occurs within 120 days after the date of authorization or the date the payment is made if it occurs more than 120 days after the date of authorization.

(6) A corporation's indebtedness to a shareholder or member that is incurred by reason of a distribution made under this section is at parity with the corporation's indebtedness to its general, unsecured creditors, except as otherwise agreed.

(7) If a corporation acquires its shares or memberships in exchange for an obligation to make future payments, and distribution of an obligation would otherwise be prohibited under subsection (3) at the time it is made, the corporation may issue the obligation and all of the following apply:

(a) The portion of the obligation that could have been distributed without violating subsection (3) is treated as indebtedness as described in subsection (6).

(b) All of the following apply to the portion of the obligation that exceeds the amount treated as indebtedness under subdivision (a):

(i) At any time before the due date of the obligation, payments of principal and interest may be made as a distribution to the extent that a distribution may then be made under this section.

(ii) At any time on or after the due date, the obligation to pay principal and interest is considered distributed and treated as indebtedness described in subsection (6) to the extent that a distribution may be made at that time under this section.

(iii) Unless otherwise provided in the agreement for the acquisition of the shares, the obligation is a liability or debt for purposes of determining whether distributions other than payments on the obligation may be made under this section, except for purposes of determining whether distributions may be made with respect to shares that have preferential rights superior to those of shares acquired in exchange for the obligation.

(8) The enforceability of a guaranty or other undertaking by a third party that relates to a distribution is not affected by the prohibition of the distribution under subsection (3).

(9) If a claim is made to recover a distribution that violates subsection (3), or if a violation of subsection (3) is raised as a defense to a claim based on a distribution, this section does not prevent the person that received the distribution from asserting a right of rescission or other legal or equitable rights.

450.2391 Conferring voting and inspection rights upon bond holders; signatures of officers.
Sec. 391.

(1) A corporation, in its articles of incorporation, may confer upon the holders of bonds issued or to be issued by it, rights to inspect the corporate books and records and to vote in the election of directors and on any other matters

on which shareholders or members of the corporation may vote to the extent, in the manner, and subject to the conditions prescribed in the articles. The articles may grant to the board the power to confer such voting or inspection rights under the terms of any bonds issued or to be issued by the corporation.

(2) The signatures of the officers upon a bond may be facsimiles.

450.2392 Applicability of chapter to distributions made in dissolution under chapter 8.
Sec. 392.

This chapter does not apply to distributions made in a dissolution under chapter 8.

Chapter 4 – Meetings and Voting

450.2401 Meetings of shareholders or members; location.
Sec. 401.

Meetings of shareholders or members may be held at a place within or without this state as provided in the bylaws. In the absence of such a provision, meetings shall be held at the registered office or such other place as may be determined by the board.

450.2402 Annual meeting of shareholders or members for election of directors and conduct other business; failure to hold meeting at designated time or elect sufficient number of directors; adjournment of meeting; court order to hold meeting or election; quorum.
Sec. 402.

A corporation shall hold an annual meeting of its shareholders or members, to elect directors and conduct any other business that may come before the meeting, on a date designated in the bylaws, unless the shareholders or members act by written consent under section 407 or by ballot under section 408 or 409. A failure to hold the annual meeting at the designated time, or to elect a sufficient number of directors at the meeting or any adjournment of the meeting, does not affect otherwise valid corporate acts or work a forfeiture or give cause for dissolution of the corporation, except as provided in section 823. If the annual meeting is not held on the date designated for the meeting, the board shall cause the meeting to be held as soon after that date as is convenient. If the annual meeting is not held for 90 days after the date designated for the meeting, or if no date is designated for 15 months after formation of the corporation or after its last annual meeting, the circuit court for the county in which the principal place of business or registered office of the corporation is located, on application of a shareholder or member, may summarily order that the corporation hold the meeting or the election, or both, and that it is held at the time and place, after the notice, and for the transaction of the business that is designated in the order. At any meeting ordered by the court under this section, the shareholders or members that are present in person or by proxy and that have voting powers constitute a quorum for transaction of the business designated in the order.

450.2403 Special meeting of shareholders or members; court order; quorum.
Sec. 403.

The board may call a special meeting of shareholders or members or the officers, directors, shareholders, or members may call a special meeting as provided in the bylaws. Notwithstanding any provision in the bylaws concerning the call of a special meeting, if it receives an application from the holders of not less than 10% of all the shares or from not less than 10% of all the members entitled to vote at a meeting, the circuit court for the county in which the principal place of business or registered office is located, for good cause shown, may order the call of a special meeting of shareholders or members and that it is held at the time and place, after the notice, and for the transaction of the business that is designated in the order. At any meeting ordered by the court under this section, the shareholders or members that are present in person or by proxy and that have voting powers constitute a quorum for transaction of the business designated in the order.

450.2404 Notice of time, place, and purposes of meeting of shareholders or members; manner; contents; notice of adjourned meeting; notice not given; attendance at meeting; participating and voting by remote communication; meeting without notice.
Sec. 404.

(1) Except as otherwise provided in this act, written notice of the time, place, if any, and purposes of a meeting of shareholders or members shall be given in any of the following manners:
  (a) Personally, by mail, or by electronic transmission, not less than 10 or more than 60 days before the date of the meeting to each shareholder or member of record that is entitled to vote at the meeting.
  (b) By including the notice, prominently displayed, in a newspaper or other periodical that is regularly published at least semiannually by or in behalf of the corporation and addressed and mailed, postage prepaid, to each member or shareholder entitled to vote at the meeting not less than 10 or more than 60 days before the meeting.
(2) A corporation may provide notice to a shareholder or member that is not or may not be entitled to vote at a meeting of shareholders or members in a manner provided in subsection (1), whether or not the notice is required under this act or under other applicable law.

(3) Notice of the purposes of a meeting shall include notice of any proposal a shareholder or member intends to propose, if that proposal is a proper subject for shareholder or member action and the shareholder or member notified the corporation in writing of the shareholder's or member's intention to present the proposal at the meeting. The bylaws may establish reasonable procedures for the submission of proposals to the corporation in advance of a meeting.

(4) If a meeting of the shareholders or members is adjourned to another time or place, it is not necessary, unless the bylaws otherwise provide, to give notice of the adjourned meeting if the time and place to which the meeting is adjourned are announced at the meeting at which the adjournment is taken. If after an adjournment the board fixes a new record date for the adjourned meeting, the corporation shall give notice of the adjourned meeting to each shareholder or member of record on the new record date that is entitled to notice under subsection (1).

(5) If a meeting of shareholders or members is adjourned under subsection (4), the shareholders or members may only transact business that they might have transacted at the original meeting at the adjourned meeting if a notice of the adjourned meeting is not given. A shareholder, member, or proxy holder may be present and vote at the adjourned meeting by a means of remote communication if that person was permitted to be present and vote by that means of remote communication in the original meeting notice.

(6) A shareholder's or member's attendance at a meeting, in person or by proxy, will result in both of the following:

    (a) Waiver of objection to lack of notice or defective notice of the meeting, unless the shareholder or member at the beginning of the meeting objects to holding the meeting or transacting business at the meeting.

    (b) Waiver of objection to consideration of a particular matter at the meeting that is not within the purpose or purposes described in the meeting notice, unless the shareholder or member objects to considering the matter when it is presented.

(7) If a shareholder, member, or proxy holder is permitted to participate in and vote at a meeting by remote communication under section 405, the notice described in subsection (1) shall include a description of the means of remote communication by which a shareholder, member, or proxy holder may participate.

(8) This section does not prohibit a corporation from conducting a meeting of its shareholders or members without notice or with the notice prescribed in the articles of incorporation or bylaws, if the meeting is for a purpose or purposes that do not involve the election of directors or the taking of other actions involving control or governance of the corporation for which a vote of the shareholders or members is required under this act, the articles of incorporation, the bylaws, or an agreement under section 488.

450.2405 Shareholder, member, or proxy holder participation in meeting by conference telephone or other means of remote communication; conditions;

participation as presence in person at meeting; participating and voting by remote communication.
Sec. 405.

(1) Unless otherwise restricted by the articles of incorporation or bylaws, a shareholder, member, or proxy holder may participate in a meeting of shareholders or members by a conference telephone or other means of remote communication that permits all persons that participate in the meeting to communicate with all the other participants. All participants shall be advised of the means of remote communication.
(2) Participation in a meeting under this section constitutes presence in person at the meeting.
(3) Unless otherwise restricted by any provisions of the articles of incorporation or bylaws, the board of directors may hold a meeting of shareholders or members that is conducted solely by means of remote communication.
(4) Subject to any guidelines and procedures adopted by the board of directors, shareholders, members, and proxy holders that are not physically present at a meeting of shareholders or members may participate in the meeting by a means of remote communication and are considered present in person and may vote at the meeting if all of the following are met:
   (a) The corporation implements reasonable measures to verify that each person that is considered present and permitted to vote at the meeting by means of remote communication is a shareholder, member, or proxy holder.
   (b) The corporation implements reasonable measures to provide each shareholder, member, or proxy holder a reasonable opportunity to participate in the meeting and to vote on matters submitted to the shareholders or members, including an opportunity to read or hear the proceedings of the meeting substantially concurrently with the proceedings.
   (c) If any shareholder, member, or proxy holder votes or takes other action at the meeting by a means of remote communication, a record of the vote or other action is maintained by the corporation.

450.2406 Chairperson presiding at meeting of shareholders or members; powers, duties, and authority.
Sec. 406.

(1) At each meeting of shareholders or members, a chairperson shall preside. The chairperson shall be appointed as provided in the bylaws or, in the absence of a provision in the bylaws, by the board of directors.
(2) Unless the articles of incorporation or bylaws provide otherwise, the chairperson that presides at a meeting of the shareholders or members shall determine the order of business and has the authority to establish rules for the conduct of the meeting. Any rules adopted for, or for the conduct of, the meeting must be fair to shareholders or members.

(3) The chairperson of a meeting shall announce at the meeting when the polls close for each vote of the shareholders or members. If an announcement is not made, the polls close on the final adjournment of the meeting. After the polls close, ballots, proxies, and votes and any revocations or changes to ballots, proxies, or votes, shall not be accepted.

450.2406a Notice by electronic transmission.
Sec. 406a.

In addition to any other form of notice to a shareholder or member permitted by the articles of incorporation, the bylaws, or this chapter, any notice given to a shareholder or member by a form of electronic transmission to which the shareholder or member has consented is effective.

450.2407 Taking corporate action without meeting; consent; notice; statement on filed certificate; consent by electronic transmission; delivery.
Sec. 407.

(1) The articles of incorporation may provide that any action the shareholders or members are required or permitted by this act to take at an annual or special meeting may be taken without a meeting, without prior notice, and without a vote, if written consents, setting forth the action taken, are signed and dated by the holders of outstanding shares or members or their proxies that have not less than the minimum number of votes that is necessary to authorize or take the action at a meeting at which all shares or members entitled to vote on the action were present and voted. The corporation shall give prompt notice of any corporate action taken without a meeting by less than unanimous written consent to those shareholders or members that did not consent to the action in writing.

(2) If the shareholders or members take an action by written consent under subsection (1) that would require filing of a certificate under any other section of this act if the action had been taken at a meeting of the shareholders or members, the certificate filed under that other section shall state, in lieu of any statement required by that section concerning a vote of shareholders or members, that both written consent and written notice have been given as provided in subsection (1).

(3) Any action the shareholders or members are required or permitted by this act to take at an annual or special meeting may be taken without a meeting, without prior notice, and without a vote, if before or after the action all the shareholders or members entitled to vote on the action or their proxies consent to the action in writing. If the shareholders or members take an action by written consent under this subsection that requires filing of a certificate under any other section of this act if the action had been taken at a meeting, the certification filed under the other section shall state, in lieu of any statement required by that section concerning a vote of the shareholders

or members, that written consent has been given as provided in this subsection.

(4) An electronic transmission that consents to an action that is transmitted by a shareholder, member, or proxy holder, or by a person authorized to act for the shareholder, member, or proxy holder, is written, signed, and dated for the purposes of this section if the electronic transmission is delivered with information from which the corporation can determine that the electronic transmission was transmitted by the shareholder, member, or proxy holder, or by a person authorized to act for the shareholder, member, or proxy holder, and the date on which the electronic transmission was transmitted. The date on which an electronic transmission is transmitted is the date on which the consent was signed for purposes of this section. A consent given by electronic transmission is not delivered until it is reproduced in paper form and the paper form is delivered to the corporation by delivery to its registered office in this state, its principal office in this state, or an officer or agent of the corporation that has custody of the book in which proceedings of meetings of shareholders or members are recorded. Delivery to a corporation's registered office shall be made by hand or by certified or registered mail, return receipt requested. Delivery to a corporation's principal office in this state or to an officer or agent of the corporation that has custody of the book in which proceedings of meetings of shareholders or members are recorded shall be made by hand, by certified or registered mail, return receipt requested, or in any other manner provided in the articles of incorporation or bylaws or by resolution of the board of directors of the corporation.

450.2408 Taking corporate action without meeting; shareholder or member action by ballot; requirements; revocation of ballot; inclusion of proposed action in ballot; statement of certificate.
Sec. 408.

(1) A corporation may provide in its articles of incorporation or in bylaws that are approved by the shareholders or members that any action the shareholders or members are required or permitted to take at an annual or special meeting, including the election of directors, may be taken without a meeting if the corporation provides a ballot to each shareholder or member that is entitled to vote on the action in the manner provided in section 404 for providing notice of meetings of shareholders or members. A provision in the articles of incorporation or bylaws authorizing shareholder or member action by ballot shall not preclude calling or holding annual or special meetings of shareholders or members.

(2) The ballot provided to shareholders or members under subsection (1) shall meet all of the following:
  (a) Set forth each proposed action.
  (b) Provide an opportunity for the shareholders or members to vote for or against each proposed action.

(c) Specify a time by which the corporation must receive a ballot in order to be counted as a vote of the shareholder or member. The time specified shall be not less than 20 or more than 90 days after the date the corporation provides the ballot to the shareholders or members.

(3) An action is considered approved by the shareholders or members by ballot if the total number of shareholders or members voting or the total number of shareholder or member votes cast in ballots received by the corporation by the time specified in the ballots equals or exceeds the quorum required to be present at a meeting to take the action, and the number of favorable votes equals or exceeds the number of votes that would be required to approve the action at a meeting at which the number of votes cast by shareholders or members present was the same as the number of votes cast by ballot. Except as otherwise provided in the articles of incorporation, an invalid ballot, an abstention, or the submission of a ballot marked "abstain" with respect to any action does not constitute a vote cast on that action.

(4) Except as otherwise provided in the articles of incorporation or bylaws, a shareholder or member may not revoke a ballot received by the corporation.

(5) Subject to subsection (6), a corporation that provides in its articles of incorporation or bylaws for shareholder or member action by ballot may establish procedures that enable shareholders or members or a specified number or percentage of shareholders or members to include proposed actions in a ballot.

(6) If holders of at least 10% of all the voting shares or of at least 10% of the member votes submit a proposal for action by the shareholders or members, a corporation that provides in its articles of incorporation or bylaws for membership action by ballot shall include the proposed action in a ballot and submit that ballot to the shareholders or members as provided in this section.

(7) If any other section of this act requires the filing of a certificate with the department if an action is approved by vote of the shareholders or members at a meeting, the shareholders or members may approve that action by ballot under subsection (1) and, in lieu of any statement required under that section concerning the vote of the shareholders or members at a meeting, the certificate shall state that the action was approved by ballot under this section.

450.2409 Taking corporate action without meeting; voting by shareholder or member at polling place; accessibility; requirements; revocation of ballot; inclusion of proposed action in ballot; statement on certificate.
Sec. 409.

(1) A corporation may provide in its articles of incorporation or in bylaws that are approved by the shareholders or members that any action the shareholders or members are required or permitted take at an annual or special meeting, including the election of directors, may be taken without a meeting if the corporation provides a ballot to each shareholder or member that is entitled to vote that allows the shareholder or member to vote at a

polling place or at polling places established by the corporation that are reasonably accessible to the shareholders or members. The corporation shall provide notice to each shareholder or member that is entitled to cast a ballot at a shareholder or member vote held at a polling place or at polling places under this subsection within the same time and in the same manner provided for notice of meetings of shareholders or members under this act. The notice shall describe each proposed action that is included on the ballot, the location of the polling place or places, and the times when the polling places are open. A provision in the articles of incorporation or bylaws that authorizes shareholder or member action by ballot cast at a polling place or at polling places does not preclude the calling or holding of an annual or special meeting of shareholders or members.

(2) A ballot authorized under subsection (1) shall describe each proposed action and provide an opportunity for a shareholder or member to vote for or against the action.

(3) An action is considered approved by the shareholders or members by ballot under this section if the total number of shareholders or members that vote or the total number of votes cast by shareholders or members at the polling place or polling places during the period when the polls were open equals or exceeds the quorum required to be present at a meeting to take that action, and the number of favorable votes equals or exceeds the number of votes that would be required to take the action at a meeting at which the number of votes cast by shareholders or members present was the same as the number of votes cast by ballot. Except as otherwise provided in the articles of incorporation, an invalid ballot, an abstention, or the submission of a ballot marked "abstain" with respect to any action does not constitute a vote cast on that action.

(4) Except as otherwise provided in the articles of incorporation or bylaws, a shareholder or member may not revoke a ballot cast at a polling place.

(5) Subject to subsection (6), a corporation that provides in its articles of incorporation or bylaws for shareholder or member action by ballot cast at a polling place or at polling places may establish procedures that enable shareholders or members or a specified number or percentage of shareholders or members to include proposed actions in a ballot.

(6) If holders of at least 10% of all the voting shares or of at least 10% of the member votes submit a proposed action by the shareholders or members, a corporation that provides in its articles of incorporation or bylaws for membership action by ballot cast at a polling place or at polling places shall include the proposed action in a ballot and submit such ballot to the shareholders or members as provided in this section.

(7) If any other section of this act requires the filing of a certificate with the department if an action is approved by vote of the shareholders or members at a meeting, the shareholders or members may approve that action by ballot under subsection (1) and, in lieu of any statement required under that section concerning the vote of the shareholders or members at a meeting, the certificate shall state that the action was approved by ballot under this section.

450.2412 Record date.
Sec. 412.

(1) Except as provided in this subsection, for the purpose of determining which
shareholders or members are entitled to notice of and to vote at a meeting of
shareholders or members, notice of an adjournment of a meeting, or notice
of or to cast a ballot at a polling place, and for the purpose of determining
the shareholders or members that are entitled to receive and to cast a ballot
under section 408, the bylaws may provide for establishing a record date,
or, in the absence of a bylaws provision, the board shall by resolution
establish a record date. If the bylaws establish a record date, the board shall
comply with the bylaws in establishing the record date. The record date
shall not precede the date on which the resolution fixing the record date is
adopted by the board. The record date shall not be more than 60 or fewer
than 10 days before the date of the meeting or the first day on which a
shareholder or member may cast a ballot at a polling place under section
409. If the vote is by ballot under section 408, the record date shall be not
more than 60 or fewer than 20 days before the last date on which the
corporation must receive the ballots for them to be counted. If a record date
is not fixed, the record date for determination of shareholders or members
entitled to notice of or to vote at a meeting of shareholders or members or to
cast a ballot at a polling place is the close of business on the day next
preceding the day on which notice is given, or if no notice is given, the day
next preceding the day on which the meeting is held or the day next
preceding the first day on which a shareholder or member may cast a ballot
at a polling place under section 409. If the vote is by ballot under section
408, and a record date is not fixed, the record date for determination of
which shareholders or members are entitled to receive and cast a ballot is
the close of business of the day next preceding the day on which the
corporation provides the ballot to the shareholders or members under
section 408(1). If a determination of which shareholders or members of
record are entitled to notice of or to vote at a meeting of shareholders or
members is made under this section, the determination applies to any
adjournment of the meeting, unless the board establishes a new record date
under this section for the adjourned meeting.

(2) For the purpose of determining which shareholders or members are entitled
to express consent to or to dissent from a proposal without a meeting under
section 407, the bylaws may provide for establishing a record date. The
record date shall not be more than 60 days before the proposed effective
date of the shareholder or member action. If the bylaws do not establish a
record date, the board may establish a record date that does not precede the
date the board adopts the resolution establishing the record date and is not
more than 10 days after the board resolution. If a record date is not
established and prior action by the board is required with respect to any
corporate action to be taken without a meeting under section 407, the record
date is the close of business on the day on which the resolution of the board
is adopted. If a record date is not fixed and prior action by the board is not

required, the record date is the first date on which a signed written consent is delivered to the corporation under section 407.

(3) For the purpose of determining shareholders or members that are entitled to receive payment of a share dividend, distribution, or allotment of a right or for the purpose of any other action, the bylaws may provide for establishing a record date, or, in the absence of a bylaws provision, the board may establish a record date. The record date shall not precede the date on which the resolution establishing the record date is adopted by the board. The date shall not be more than 60 days before the payment of the share dividend, distribution, or allotment of a right or other action. If a record date is not established, the record date is the close of business on the day on which the resolution of the board relating to the corporate action is adopted.

450.2413 Making and certifying list of shareholders or members entitled to vote at meeting or adjournment; requirements; noncompliance; adjournment of meeting; validity of action taken.
Sec. 413.

(1) The officer or agent responsible for the shareholder or membership records of a corporation shall make and certify a complete list of the shareholders or members entitled to vote at a meeting or any adjourned meeting of the shareholders or members. All of the following apply to the list:
  (a) The officer or agent shall arrange the list alphabetically within each class and include the address of each member or shareholder and, if applicable, the number of shares held by each shareholder.
  (b) The officer or agent shall produce the list at the time and place of the meeting.
  (c) The list is open to examination by any shareholder or member during the entire meeting. If the meeting is held solely by means of remote communication, then the officer or agent shall make the list open to the examination of any shareholder or member during the entire meeting by posting the list on a reasonably accessible electronic network, and providing the information required to access the list with the notice of the meeting.
  (d) The list is prima facie evidence of which shareholders or members are entitled to examine the list or to vote at the meeting.
(2) If the requirements of this section are not complied with, and a shareholder or member that is present in person or by proxy in good faith challenges the existence of sufficient votes to approve any action at the meeting, the corporation shall adjourn the meeting until the requirements are complied with. Failure to comply with the requirements of this section does not affect the validity of an action taken at the meeting before a challenge under this subsection.

450.2415 Quorum; continuing conduct of business if less than quorum; adjournment of meeting; shareholders entitled to vote separately.
Sec. 415.

(1) Unless a greater or lesser quorum is provided in the articles of incorporation, in a bylaw adopted by the shareholders, members, or incorporators, or in this act, shares or members entitled to cast a majority of the votes at a meeting constitute a quorum at the meeting. If the withdrawal of shareholders or members leaves less than a quorum before adjournment, the remaining shareholders or members present in person or by proxy at the meeting may continue to do business until adjournment. Whether or not a quorum is present, a meeting may be adjourned by a vote of the shareholders or members present.
(2) If the holders of a class of shares or members of a class are entitled to vote separately on an item of business, this section applies in determining the presence of a quorum of the class for transaction of the item of business.

450.2421 Authorizing person to act for shareholder or member by proxy; election of directors by proxy; validity; revocability; methods of granting authority; use of copy, facsimile, or reproduction.
Sec. 421.

(1) Except as otherwise provided by statute, in the articles of incorporation, or in a bylaw that is adopted by the shareholders or members of a corporation organized on a stock or membership basis, a shareholder or member that is entitled to vote at a meeting of shareholders or members, to cast a ballot under section 408 or 409, or to express consent or dissent without a meeting may authorize other persons to act for the shareholder or member by proxy. Except as otherwise provided by statute, in the articles of incorporation, or in a bylaw, a director or other person that is entitled to vote in the election of directors of a corporation organized on a directorship basis may authorize another person or persons to act for the director or other person with respect to the election of directors by proxy.
(2) A proxy is not valid after the expiration of 3 years from its date unless otherwise provided in the proxy.
(3) A proxy is revocable at the pleasure of the person that executes it, except as otherwise provided in this section and sections 422 and 423.
(4) The authority of the holder of a proxy to act is not revoked by the incompetence or death of the person who executed the proxy unless, before the authority is exercised, written notice of an adjudication of the incompetence or death is received by the corporate officer that is responsible for maintaining the list of shareholders, members, or persons that are entitled to vote in the election of directors of a directorship corporation.
(5) Without limiting the manner in which a shareholder, member, or person that is entitled to vote in the election of directors of a directorship corporation may authorize another person or persons to act as proxy for the shareholder,

member, or person under subsection (1), each of the following methods constitute a valid means by which a shareholder, member, or person entitled to vote in the election of directors of a directorship corporation may grant authority to another person to act as proxy:

(a) Delivering a writing to the person that authorizes that person to act for the shareholder, member, or person entitled to vote in the election of directors of a directorship corporation as proxy and is executed by the shareholder, member, or person entitled to vote in the election of directors of a directorship corporation, or by an authorized officer, director, employee, or agent of the shareholder, member, or person entitled to vote in the election of directors of a directorship corporation, by signing the writing or causing his or her signature to be affixed to the writing by any reasonable means, including, but not limited to, facsimile signature.

(b) Transmitting or authorizing the transmission of a telegram, cablegram, or other means of electronic transmission to the person that will hold the proxy; or to a proxy solicitation firm, proxy support service organization, or similar agent that the person who will hold the proxy authorized to receive that transmission on the person's behalf. Any telegram, cablegram, or other means of electronic transmission must either set forth or include with it information from which it can be determined that the telegram, cablegram, or other electronic transmission was authorized by the shareholder, member, or person entitled to vote in the election of directors of a directorship corporation. If a telegram, cablegram, or other electronic transmission is determined to be valid, the inspectors or, if there are no inspectors, the persons making the determination shall specify the information on which they relied.

(6) A copy, facsimile telecommunication, or other reliable reproduction of the writing or transmission created under subsection (5) may be substituted or used in lieu of the original writing or transmission for any purpose for which the original writing or transmission could be used, if the copy, facsimile telecommunication, or other reproduction is a complete reproduction of the entire original writing or transmission.

450.2422 Irrevocable proxy.
Sec. 422.

A proxy that is entitled "irrevocable proxy", and that states that it is irrevocable, is irrevocable when it is held by any of the following or a nominee of any of the following:

(a) In the case of shares or memberships that are transferable, a holder of a pledge or other security interest in the shares or membership.

(b) In the case of shares or memberships that are transferable, a person that has purchased or agreed to purchase the shares or membership.

(c) A creditor of the corporation that extends or continues credit to the corporation in consideration of the proxy.

(d) An individual who has contracted to perform services as a director, officer, or employee of the corporation, if a proxy is required by the contract of employment.

(e) A person designated by or under an agreement under section 461.

(f) A holder of any other proxy coupled with an interest.

450.2423 Revocability of proxy.
Sec. 423.

(1) A proxy described in section 422 becomes revocable, notwithstanding a provision that makes it irrevocable, after the pledge is redeemed, the security interest is terminated, the debt of the corporation is paid, the period of employment provided for in the contract of employment expires, or the agreement under section 461 is terminated. A proxy described in section 422(c) or (d) is revocable 3 years after the date of the proxy or at the end of any period specified in the proxy, whichever period is less, unless the period of irrevocability is renewed by execution of a new irrevocable proxy. This subsection does not affect the duration of a proxy under section 421(2).

(2) A proxy is revocable, notwithstanding a provision that makes it irrevocable, by a purchaser of shares that did not know at the time of purchase of the existence of the provision unless the existence of the proxy and its irrevocability are noted conspicuously on the face or back of the certificate representing the shares.

450.2431 Inspectors at shareholders' or members' meeting; waiver; appointment and duties; failure to appoint; vacancy; report; evidence.
Sec. 431.

(1) If the bylaws require inspectors at a shareholders' or members' meeting, the requirement is waived unless compliance therewith is requested by a shareholder or member present in person or by proxy and entitled to vote at the meeting. Unless otherwise provided in the bylaws, the board, in advance of a shareholders' or members' meeting, may appoint 1 or more inspectors to act at the meeting or any adjournment thereof. If inspectors are not so appointed, the person presiding at a shareholders' or members' meeting may, and on request of a shareholder or member entitled to vote shall, appoint 1 or more inspectors. In case a person appointed fails to appear or act, the vacancy may be filled by appointment made by the board in advance of the meeting or at the meeting by the person presiding.

(2) The inspectors shall determine the number of shares outstanding and the voting power of each or the members entitled to vote, the shares or members entitled to vote represented at the meeting, the existence of a quorum, the validity and effect of proxies, and shall receive votes, ballots or consents, hear and determine challenges and questions arising in connection with the right to vote, count and tabulate votes, ballots or consents, determine the result, and do such acts as are proper to conduct the election

or vote with fairness to all shareholders or members. On request of the person presiding at the meeting or a shareholder or member entitled to vote, the inspectors shall make and execute a written report to the person presiding at the meeting of any of the facts found by them and matters determined by them. The report is prima facie evidence of the facts stated and of the vote as certified by the inspectors.

450.2432 Beneficial owner of shares or memberships registered in name of nominee; recognition by corporation as shareholder or member; procedure.
Sec. 432.

(1) A corporation may establish a procedure under which the beneficial owner of shares or memberships that are registered in the name of a nominee is recognized by the corporation as the shareholder or member. The procedure established may determine the extent of this recognition.
(2) A procedure established under subsection (1) may include any of the following:
    (a) The type of nominees to which it applies.
    (b) The rights or privileges that the corporation recognizes in the beneficial owner.
    (c) The manner in which the procedure is selected by the nominee.
    (d) The information that the nominee, shareholder, or member must provide if the procedure is selected.
    (e) The period for which selection of the procedure is effective.
    (f) Other aspects of the rights and duties created.

450.2441 Voting generally.
Sec. 441.

(1) Each outstanding share or member is entitled to 1 vote on each matter submitted to a vote, unless otherwise provided under section 303 or 304. A person may cast a vote at a meeting of the shareholders or members either orally or in writing, unless otherwise provided in the bylaws.
(2) If an action, other than the election of directors, is submitted for a vote of the shareholders or members, the action is approved or authorized if it receives the affirmative vote of a majority of the votes cast by the holders of shares or members entitled to vote on the action, unless a higher vote is required in the articles of incorporation or a higher or lower vote is required under another section of this act. Unless otherwise provided by the articles of incorporation, abstaining from a vote or submitting a ballot marked "abstain" with respect to an action is not a vote cast on that action. Except as otherwise provided in the articles of incorporation, directors are elected by a plurality of the votes cast at an election.

450.2442 Voting as class.
Sec. 442.

(1) The articles of incorporation or bylaws may provide that a class of shares or members shall vote as a class to authorize any action, including amendment to the articles of incorporation. A vote as a class under this section is in addition to any other vote required under this act. If voting as a class is provided in the articles of incorporation or bylaws, it shall be by the proportionate vote provided in the articles of incorporation or bylaws or, if a proportionate vote is not so provided, then for any action other than the election of directors, by a majority of the votes cast by the holders of shares or members of the class entitled to vote on the action.

(2) If voting as a class is required under this act to authorize an action, the action is authorized if it receives the affirmative vote of a majority of the votes cast by the shareholders or members of each class entitled to vote on that action, unless a higher vote is required in the articles of incorporation or under another section of this act. A vote as a class under this subsection is in addition to any other vote required under this act.

(3) Unless otherwise provided in the articles of incorporation, abstaining from a vote or submitting a ballot marked "abstain" with respect to an action that requires authorization by a class of shareholders or members is not a vote cast on that action.

450.2443 Grouping of members in local units; basis; purpose; actions authorized by bylaws; incorporation and powers of local units; powers, rights, and privileges of elected representatives or delegates.
Sec. 443.

(1) The articles of incorporation or bylaws adopted by the members of a nonstock corporation may provide that members or a class or classes of members shall be grouped in local units, formed upon the basis of territorial units or some other reasonable basis, for the purpose of election of delegates or representatives to represent the members or the class or classes of members within such local units at any annual or special meeting or for the purpose of election of members to the board of directors.

(2) If the articles of incorporation or bylaws authorize the grouping of members in local units, the bylaws shall do, or shall authorize the board to do, the following:

    (a) Draw the local units according to the territorial limits or other reasonable basis.

    (b) Only if the grouping is for the purpose of election of delegates, determine the number of delegates to which members or each class of members within the local units are entitled, in accordance with the members' respective voting rights. Members or any class of members within each local unit who do not have voting rights shall be entitled to at least 1 delegate. Unless the articles of incorporation or bylaws otherwise provide, a delegate representing members or any class of members who do not have voting rights shall not have voting rights.

(c) Take other actions reasonably necessary to insure the fair representation of each member within the local units at meetings of the corporation.

(3) The local units designated pursuant to this section may be incorporated under the laws of this state by the members of the local unit, and may do all things necessary to give effect to the preceding sections, the rules promulgated, and bylaws adopted under this act.

(4) Representatives or delegates elected pursuant to this section shall have and may exercise all of the powers, rights, and privileges of members at an annual or special meeting, subject in all respects to the provisions of this act governing members.

450.2444 Voting by corporation or business corporation; voting of pledged shares.
Sec. 444.

(1) Shares or memberships that are held by another domestic corporation, domestic business corporation, foreign corporation, or foreign business corporation, whether or not the corporation or business corporation is subject to this act, may be voted by an officer or agent, or by a proxy that is appointed by an officer or agent or by some other person, who by action of its board or under its bylaws is appointed to vote the shares or membership.

(2) A shareholder whose shares are pledged is entitled to vote the shares until they are transferred into the name of the pledgee or a nominee of the pledgee.

450.2445 Voting of shares or membership held by person in representative or fiduciary capacity or held jointly by fiduciaries.
Sec. 445.

(1) The vote of shares or a membership held by a person in a representative or fiduciary capacity may be cast by that person without a transfer of the shares or membership into the name of the representative or fiduciary.

(2) The vote of shares or a membership held jointly by fiduciaries, where the instrument or order appointing the fiduciaries does not otherwise direct, shall be cast as follows:

(a) If only 1 fiduciary votes, that act binds all.

(b) If more than 1 fiduciary votes, the vote of the shares or membership shall be cast as the majority of the fiduciaries determines.

(c) If the fiduciaries ae equally divided as to how the vote of the shares or membership shall be cast, a court having jurisdiction in an action brought by any of the fiduciaries or by any beneficiary may appoint an additional person to act with the fiduciaries in such matter, and the vote

of the stock or membership shall be cast by the majority of such
fiduciaries and such additional person.

450.2446 Voting of shares or membership held by joint tenants or tenants in common.
Sec. 446.

Shares or a membership that are held by 2 or more persons as joint tenants or as
tenants in common may be voted at a meeting of shareholders or members or by
ballot under section 408 or 409 by any joint tenant or tenant in common, unless
another joint tenant or tenant in common seeks to vote the shares or membership
in person or by proxy. In the latter event, the written agreement, if any, that
governs the manner in which the shares or membership are voted, controls if
presented at the meeting, either physically or by means of electronic
transmission or if presented to the corporation either physically or by means of
electronic transmission before the time for casting a ballot under section 408 or
409 expires. If an agreement that governs votes is not presented at the meeting,
the majority in interest of the joint tenants or tenants in common present
determines the manner of voting. In the case of a stock corporation or a
membership that carries more than 1 vote, if there is no majority in interest of
the joint tenants or tenants in common present, the shares or member votes, for
the purpose of voting, shall be divided among those joint tenants or tenants in
common that are present in person in accordance with their interest in the shares
or membership.

450.2447a Voting of shares or memberships if owned by another corporation or business corporation.
Sec. 447a.

Unless specifically otherwise provided in the articles of incorporation or bylaws,
absent an order of a court of competent jurisdiction based on a determination
that special circumstances exist and the best interests of the corporation would
be served, the shares or memberships of a corporation shall not be voted on any
matter or considered to be outstanding shares or memberships for any purpose
related to voting if they are owned, directly or indirectly, by another corporation,
foreign corporation, business corporation, or foreign business corporation, and
the first corporation owns, directly or indirectly, a majority of the shares or
memberships entitled to vote for directors of the second corporation.

450.2448 Redemption of shares; voting.
Sec. 448.

After written notice of redemption of redeemable shares has been mailed to the
holders thereof and a sum sufficient to redeem the shares has been deposited
with a bank or trust company with irrevocable instruction and authority to pay

the redemption price to the holders thereof upon surrender of certificates therefor, the shares shall not be voted on any matter nor deemed to be outstanding shares.

450.2451 Voting for directors.
Sec. 451.

(1) The articles of incorporation of a corporation that is organized on a stock or membership basis may provide that a shareholder or member that is entitled to vote at an election for directors may vote, in person, by proxy, or by ballot as provided in section 408 or 409, for as many individuals as there are directors to be elected and for whose election the shareholder or member has a right to vote, or to cumulate votes by giving 1 candidate as many votes as the number of directors to be elected multiplied by the number of votes held by the shareholder or member, or by distributing the votes of the shareholder or member on the same principle among any number of the candidates.

(2) The articles of incorporation of a corporation that is organized on a directorship basis may provide that a person that is entitled to vote at an election for directors may vote, in person, by proxy, or by electronic transmission, for as many individuals as there are directors to be elected and for whose election the person has a right to vote, or to cumulate votes by giving 1 candidate as many votes and the number of directors to be elected multiplied by the number of votes held by the person, or by distributing the votes of the person on the same principle among any number of the candidates.

450.2455 Action requiring vote or concurrence of greater proportion of shares, members, or class than required by act; amendment of articles of incorporation.
Sec. 455.

With respect to an action to be taken by the shareholders or members, if the articles of incorporation require the vote or concurrence of the holders of a greater proportion of the shares or a greater proportion of members, or of a class of shares or members, than required under this act with respect to the action, the articles of incorporation shall control. An amendment of the articles of incorporation that adds, changes, or deletes that provision requires the same vote that is required to amend the articles of incorporation under section 611, or the same vote that would be required to take action under that provision, whichever is greater. A failure to include a provision described in this section in the articles of incorporation does not invalidate any bylaw or agreement that would otherwise be considered valid.

450.2461 Agreement as to voting rights.
Sec. 461.

An agreement between 2 or more shareholders or members, if it is in writing and signed by the parties, may provide that in exercising voting rights, they shall cast their votes as provided in the agreement, or as they agree, or as determined under a procedure agreed on by them. A voting agreement executed under this section, whether or not proxies are executed under that agreement, is not subject to sections 466 to 468. A voting agreement under this section is specifically enforceable.

450.2466 Transfer of shares or membership to trustee; filing of voting rights agreement; voting and other rights of trustee; inspection of filed copy of voting trust agreement; description of beneficial interests.
Sec. 466.

(1) If shares or memberships of a corporation are transferable, a shareholder or member may confer on a trustee the right to vote or otherwise represent those shares or memberships for a period that does not exceed 10 years, by entering into a written voting trust agreement that includes the terms and conditions of the voting trust, by filing an executed counterpart of the agreement at the registered office of the corporation, and by transferring those shares or membership to the trustee for purposes of the agreement.

(2) If a voting rights agreement under subsection (1) is filed, the holder of any certificates for shares or memberships transferred shall surrender the certificates and the corporation shall cancel the certificates and issue new certificates for the shares or memberships to the trustee that state that they are issued under the agreement. The corporation shall also describe the transfer of ownership in the records of the corporation, and the trustee may vote the transferred shares or memberships during the term of the agreement.

(3) A trustee that holds memberships transferred under an agreement executed under this section has the same voting and other rights as the beneficiaries would have if the memberships were not in trust.

(4) The filed copy of a voting trust agreement under this section is subject to inspection at any reasonable time by a shareholder, member, or a holder of a beneficial interest in the voting trust, in person or by agent or attorney.

(5) Any voting trust certificates issued under subsection (2) shall describe the beneficial interests in the voting trust.

450.2467 Shares or memberships subject to voting trust; liability of trustee; designation of 2 or more persons as voting trustees.
Sec. 467.

(1) A trustee that votes shares or memberships that are subject to a voting trust under section 466 is not liable as a shareholder, member, trustee or otherwise, except for the trustee's malfeasance.
(2) If 2 or more persons are designated as voting trustees, and the right and method of voting shares or memberships in their names are not fixed in the agreement that appoints the trustees, a majority of the trustees shall determine the right to vote and manner of voting the shares or memberships. If the trustees are equally divided concerning the right to vote and the manner of voting, the votes shall be divided equally among the trustees.

450.2468 Extension of voting trust agreement.
Sec. 468.

(1) At any time within the 12-month period before the expiration of the original term of a voting trust agreement under section 466 or an extension of a voting trust agreement under this section, 1 or more beneficiaries of the voting trust, by written agreement and with written consent of the voting trustees, may extend the duration of the voting trust agreement with regard to the shares or memberships subject to their beneficial interest for an additional period that does not exceed 10 years. Before expiration of the original term of a voting trust agreement under section 466 or an extension of a voting trust agreement under this section, if the voting trustees file in the registered office of the corporation an executed counterpart of an extension agreement and of their consent to the extension, the term of the voting trust agreement is extended for the period described in the extension agreement. An extension agreement does not affect the rights or obligations of persons that are not parties to the extension agreement.
(2) If the term of an extension agreement described in subsection (1) or a voting trust agreement that otherwise meets the requirements of this act is more than 10 years, the voting trust agreement or extension agreement is valid for a period of 10 years from the date of its commencement and becomes inoperative at the end of that 10-year period unless extended under subsection (1).

450.2471 Shares as personal property; transfer; applicability of MCL 440.8101 to 440.8601.
Sec. 471.

The shares of a corporation are personal property. Article 8 of the uniform commercial code, 1962 PA 174, MCL 440.8101 to 440.8601, applies to the transfer of shares only to the extent not inconsistent with this act.

450.2472 Transfer or registration of bond, share, or membership; written restriction.
Sec. 472.

(1) The articles of incorporation, the bylaws, or an agreement among any number of holders of bonds, shares, or memberships, or among the holders and the corporation, may contain a restriction on the transfer or registration of a bond, share, or membership of a corporation that is otherwise transferable. A restriction described in this subsection is not binding with respect to bonds, shares, or memberships that are issued before adoption of the restriction unless the holders are parties to an agreement or voted in favor of the restriction.

(2) A written restriction on the transfer or registration of a bond, share, or membership of a corporation that is otherwise transferable, if permitted under this section or section 473 and noted conspicuously on the face or back of the instrument or on the information statement required under section 336, may be enforced against the holder of the restricted instrument or a successor or transferee of the holder of the restricted instrument including, but not limited to, a personal representative, administrator, trustee, guardian, or other fiduciary entrusted with similar responsibility for the person or estate of the holder. If the existence of the restriction is not noted conspicuously on the face or back of the instrument or on the information statement required under section 336, the restriction, even if permitted under this section or section 473, is ineffective except against any person that has actual knowledge of the restriction.

450.2473 Transfer or registration of bond, share, or membership; imposition of restrictions; conditions.
Sec. 473.

Without limiting the general authority under section 472(1) to impose restrictions on the transfer or registration of bonds, shares, or memberships of a corporation that are otherwise transferable, a restriction on the transfer or registration of transfer of bonds, shares, or memberships of a corporation that is consistent with section 301 is permitted if it does any of the following:

(a) Obligates the holders of the restricted instruments to offer to the corporation or to any other holders of bonds, shares or memberships of the corporation, to any other person, or to any combination of those persons, a prior opportunity to acquire the restricted instruments.

(b) Obligates the corporation or a holder of bonds, shares, or memberships of the corporation, any other person, or any combination of those persons, to purchase the instruments that are the subject of an agreement respecting the purchase and sale of the restricted instruments.

(c) Requires the corporation or the holders of a class of bonds, shares, or memberships of the corporation to consent to a proposed transfer of the restricted instruments or to approve the proposed transferee of the restricted instruments.

(d) Prohibits the transfer of the restricted instruments to designated persons or classes of persons, and the designation is not contrary to public policy.

(e) Exists for the purpose of maintaining the status of the corporation under section 115, 501, 521, 527, or 528 of the internal revenue code of 1986, 26 USC 115, 501, 521, 527, and 528.

450.2485 Books, records, and minutes.
Sec. 485.

A corporation shall keep books and records of account and minutes of the proceedings of its shareholders or members, board, and executive committee, if any. Unless otherwise provided in the bylaws, the corporation may keep the books, records, and minutes outside this state. The corporation shall keep at its registered office, or at the office of its transfer agent in or outside this state, records that contain the names and addresses of all shareholders or members, the number and class of shares held by each shareholder or the class or classes of membership held by each member, and the dates when they respectively became shareholders of record or members. Any of the books, records, or minutes may be in written form or in any other form that is convertible into written form within a reasonable time. A corporation shall convert into written form without charge any record that is not in written form, if requested by a person that is entitled to inspect the record.

450.2487 Mailing balance sheet and statements to shareholder or member upon request; inspection during regular business hours; written demand; "proper purpose" defined; order compelling inspection; burden of proof; powers of court; inspection by director; costs; holder of voting trust certificate as shareholder or member; right to inspect prohibited or limited; definitions.
Sec. 487.

(1) If requested in writing by a shareholder or member, a corporation shall mail to the shareholder or member its balance sheet as at the end of the preceding fiscal year; its statement of income for that fiscal year; and, if prepared by the corporation, its statement of source and application of funds for that fiscal year.

(2) Any shareholder or member of record of a corporation that is organized on a stock or membership basis, in person or by attorney or other agent, may during regular business hours inspect for any proper purpose the corporation's stock ledger, a list of its shareholders or members, and its other books and records, if the shareholder or member gives the corporation written demand describing with reasonable particularity the purpose of the inspection and the records the shareholder or member desires to inspect, and

the records sought are directly connected with the purpose. As used in this subsection, "proper purpose" means a purpose that is reasonably related to a person's interest as a shareholder or member. A shareholder or member must deliver a demand under this subsection to the corporation at its registered office in this state or at its principal place of business. If an attorney or other agent is the person seeking to inspect the records, the demand must include a power of attorney or other writing that authorizes the attorney or other agent to act on behalf of the shareholder or member.

(3) If a corporation does not permit an inspection required under subsection (2) within 5 business days after a demand is received under subsection (2), or imposes unreasonable conditions on the inspection, the shareholder or member may apply to the circuit court for the county in which the principal place of business or registered office of the corporation is located for an order to compel the inspection. If the shareholder or member seeks to inspect the books and records other than its stock ledger or list of shareholders or members, the shareholder or member must establish that the shareholder or member has complied with this section concerning the form and manner of making demand for inspection of the documents, that the inspection is for a proper purpose, and that the documents sought are directly connected with the purpose. If the shareholder or member seeks to inspect the corporation's stock ledger or list of shareholders or members and establishes that the stockholder or member has complied with this section concerning the form and manner of making demand for the inspection of the documents, the corporation has the burden of proof to establish that the inspection that is sought is for an improper purpose or that the records sought are not directly connected with the person's purpose. In its discretion, the court may order the corporation to permit the shareholder or member to inspect the corporation's stock ledger, a list of shareholders or members, and its other books and records, prescribe conditions and limitations on the inspection, and award other or further relief that the court considers just and proper. The court may order books, documents and records, pertinent extracts, or duly authenticated copies to be brought to this state and kept in this state and prescribe terms and conditions on those obligations.

(4) A director may examine any of the corporation's books and records for a purpose reasonably related to his or her position as a director. The director may apply to the circuit court of the county in which the principal place of business or registered office of the corporation is located for an order to compel the inspection. In its discretion, the court may order the corporation to permit the director to inspect any and all books and records, prescribe conditions and limitations on the inspection, and award other and further relief that the court considers just and proper.

(5) If the court orders inspection of the records demanded under subsection (3) or (4), it shall also order the corporation to pay the shareholder's, member's, or director's costs, including reasonable attorney fees, incurred to obtain the order unless the corporation proves that it failed to permit the inspection in

good faith because it had a reasonable basis to doubt the right of the shareholder, member, or director to inspect the records demanded.

(6) A holder of a voting trust certificate representing shares of, or membership in, the corporation is considered a shareholder or member for purposes of this section and section 485.

(7) Notwithstanding any other provisions of this act, the articles of incorporation, the bylaws, or a resolution of the board of directors may provide that the shareholders or members and attorneys or agents for shareholders or members do not have the right to inspect the corporation's stock ledger, lists of shareholder or members, lists of donors or donations, or its other books and records, if the incorporators, shareholders, members, or directors that approve a limitation under this subsection make a good faith determination that 1 or more of the following apply:

(a) Opening the stock ledger, lists of shareholder or members, lists of donors or donations, or its other books and records for inspection would impair the rights of privacy or free association of the shareholders or members.

(b) Opening the stock ledger, lists of shareholder or members, lists of donors or donations, or its other books and records for inspection would impair the lawful purposes of the corporation.

(c) Opening lists of donors or donations for inspection is not in the best interests of the corporation or its donors.

(8) A corporation that limits inspection of lists of its shareholders or members under subsection (7) shall provide a reasonable way for shareholders or members to communicate with all other shareholders or members concerning the election of directors and other affairs of the corporation. A corporation described in this subsection may require a shareholder or member that wishes to communicate with other shareholders or members under this subsection to pay the reasonable costs to cover the cost of labor and materials and third-party charges incurred by the corporation in doing so.

(9) As used in this section:

(a) "Proper purpose" means a purpose that is reasonably related to a person's interest as a shareholder or member of a corporation.

(b) "Right to inspect records" includes the right to copy and make extracts from the records of a corporation and, if reasonable, the right to require the corporation to supply copies made by photographic, xerographic, or other means. To cover the cost of labor and material, the corporation may require a shareholder or member to pay a reasonable charge for copies of the documents provided to the shareholder or member.

450.2488 Agreement among members of corporation.
Sec. 488.

(1) Subject to subsection (11), an agreement among the members of a corporation that is organized on a membership basis, among the shareholders of a corporation that is organized on a stock basis, or among

the directors of a corporation that is organized on a directorship basis that complies with this section is effective among the members, shareholders, or directors and the corporation even though it is inconsistent with this act in 1 or more of the following ways:

(a) It restricts the discretion or powers of the board.

(b) It governs the authorization or making of distributions permitted under section 301 whether or not in proportion to the membership interest or shares held, subject to limitations in sections 345 and 855 pertaining to the protection of creditors.

(c) It establishes who shall be directors or officers of the corporation, or the terms of office or manner of selection or removal of directors or officers of the corporation.

(d) In general or in regard to specific matters, it governs the exercise or division of voting power by or between the members or shareholders and directors or by or among any of the members, shareholders, or directors, including, but not limited to, use of weighted voting rights or restrictions on the voting rights of particular members, shareholders, or directors.

(e) It establishes the terms and conditions of any agreement for the transfer or use of property or the provision of services between the corporation and any member, shareholder, director, officer, or employee of the corporation or among the members, shareholders, directors, officers, or employees of the corporation.

(f) It transfers to 1 or more members, shareholders, or other persons all or part of the authority to exercise the corporate powers or to manage the business and affairs of the corporation, including, but not limited to, the resolution of any issue about which there exists a deadlock among directors, members, or shareholders.

(g) It requires dissolution of the corporation at the request of 1 or more of the members, shareholders, or directors or if a specified event or contingency occurs.

(h) It establishes that shares or memberships may be assessable by the corporation, including the procedures for an assessment and the consequences of a failure by a shareholder or member to pay an assessment.

(i) It otherwise governs the exercise of the corporate powers or the management of the business and affairs of the corporation or the relationship among the shareholders, the members, the directors, and the corporation, or among any of the shareholders, members, or directors, and is not contrary to public policy.

(2) An agreement that is authorized under this section shall meet both of the following requirements:

(a) It is included in either of the following:

(i) A provision of the articles of incorporation or bylaws that is approved by all members or shareholders or all directors of a corporation that is organized on a directorship basis at the time of the agreement.

      (ii) A written agreement that is signed by all members or shareholders or all directors of a corporation that is organized on a directorship basis at the time of the agreement and that is disclosed to the corporation.

  (b) Is subject to amendment only by all members or shareholders or by all directors of a corporation that is organized on a directorship basis at the time of the amendment, unless the agreement provides otherwise or the amendment involves a provision of the articles of incorporation described in section 209(1)(f).

(3) A corporation shall conspicuously note the existence of an agreement authorized under this section on the face or back of any certificate of membership or for shares issued by the corporation or on the information statement required under section 336. If at the time of the agreement the corporation has memberships or shares outstanding represented by certificates, the corporation shall recall the outstanding certificates and issue substitute certificates that comply with this subsection. A failure to note the existence of the agreement on the certificate or information statement does not affect the validity of the agreement or any action taken under the agreement.

(4) Any person that becomes a member of a corporation organized on a membership basis, a shareholder of a corporation organized on a stock basis, or a director of a corporation organized on a directorship basis and did not have knowledge of the existence of an agreement authorized under this section at the time the person became a member, shareholder, or director, may elect to resign as a member, shareholder, or director, may elect to rescind the transfer of any membership or shares, or may elect to maintain an action to terminate the agreement. For purposes of this subsection, a person is considered to have knowledge of an agreement authorized under this section if at the time the person becomes a member, shareholder, or director, the agreement is included in the articles of incorporation or bylaws, the agreement's existence is noted on the certificate or information statement provided under subsection (3), or a copy or a written summary of the agreement is furnished to the person before the person becomes a member, shareholder, or director. A person must commence an action to enforce a right of rescission or to terminate the agreement within 90 days after discovery of the existence of the agreement or 2 years after the person becomes a shareholder, member, or director, whichever is earlier. In an action or suit to terminate the agreement, the court in which the action is brought shall terminate the agreement if the court determines that the agreement is materially inconsistent with or detrimental to carrying out the purposes of the corporation, materially impairs rights or interests the person that brought the action or suit would reasonably have expected to have acquired in becoming a member, shareholder, or director, or is inconsistent with 1 or more of the limitations under subsection (11).

(5) If an agreement authorized in this section ceases to be effective for any reason and is contained or referred to in the corporation's articles of

incorporation or bylaws, the board may without shareholder or member action adopt an amendment to the articles of incorporation or bylaws to delete the agreement and any references to it.

(6) An agreement authorized under this section that limits the discretion or powers of the board shall relieve the directors of, and impose on the person or persons in which the discretion or powers are vested, liability for acts or omissions imposed by law on directors to the extent that the discretion or powers of the directors are limited by the agreement. The person or persons in which the discretion or powers are vested are treated as a director or directors for purposes of any indemnification and any limitation on liability under section 209.

(7) The existence or performance of an agreement authorized under this section is not grounds for imposing personal liability on any member, shareholder, or other person for the acts or debts of the corporation or for treating the corporation as if it were a partnership or unincorporated entity, even if the agreement or its performance results in failure to observe the corporate formalities otherwise applicable to the matters governed by the agreement.

(8) Filing a certificate of dissolution under section 805 is required to implement a dissolution under an agreement authorized under subsection (1)(g).

(9) Incorporators or subscribers for memberships or shares may act as members or shareholders with respect to an agreement authorized under this section if the corporation has not issued memberships or shares at the time the agreement is made.

(10) A failure to satisfy the unanimity requirement of subsection (2) with respect to an agreement authorized under this section does not invalidate any agreement or any provision of the articles of incorporation or bylaws that would otherwise be valid.

(11) An agreement under this section is not effective to do any of the following:
   (a) To authorize distributions that are not permitted under section 301.
   (b) To allow property that is held for charitable or other public purposes to be used for private benefit, through the payment or excessive compensation for goods or services, or in any other manner.
   (c) To allow the use of corporate property in a manner that is materially inconsistent with the purposes of the corporation or a valid restriction imposed by donors.

450.2489 Court action that certain acts illegal, fraudulent, or willfully unfair and oppressive; order or relief; "willfully unfair and oppressive conduct" defined.
Sec. 489.

(1) A director of a corporation that is organized on a directorship basis, a shareholder of a corporation that is organized on a stock basis, or a member of a corporation that is organized on a membership basis may bring an action in the circuit court of the county in which the principal place of business or registered office of the corporation is located to establish that the acts of the directors, shareholders, members, or others in control of the

corporation are illegal, fraudulent, or willfully unfair and oppressive to the corporation or to the director, member, or shareholder. If the director, member, or shareholder establishes grounds for relief, the circuit court may make an order or grant relief as it considers appropriate including, but not limited to, an order that provides for any of the following:

(a) The dissolution and liquidation of the assets and affairs of the corporation.

(b) The cancellation or alteration of a provision contained in the articles of incorporation, an amendment of the articles of incorporation, or the bylaws of the corporation.

(c) The cancellation of, alteration of, or an injunction against a resolution or other act of the corporation.

(d) The direction or prohibition of an act of the corporation or of shareholders, members, directors, officers, or other persons that are parties to the action.

(e) The purchase at fair value of the shares of a shareholder or the membership of a member, either by the corporation or by the officers, directors, or other shareholders or members responsible for the wrongful acts. In establishing the fair value of the shares or membership for purposes of this subsection, a shareholder or member is not considered to have any interest in charitable or other assets of the corporation that would not be distributable to shareholders or members of the corporation in a dissolution under section 855.

(f) An award of damages to the corporation or a shareholder or member. A person must commence an action seeking an award of damages within 3 years after the cause of action under this section has accrued, or within 2 years after the shareholder or member discovers or reasonably should have discovered the cause of action under this section, whichever occurs first. In awarding damages under this subsection to a shareholder or member, the shareholder or member is not considered to have any interest in charitable or other assets of the corporation that would not be distributable to shareholders or members of the corporation in a dissolution under section 855.

(2) As used in this section, "willfully unfair and oppressive conduct" with respect to a member or shareholder means a continuing course of conduct or a significant action or series of actions that substantially interferes with the rights or interests of the member or shareholder as a member or shareholder. The term does not include conduct or actions that are permitted by an agreement, the articles of incorporation, the bylaws, or a consistently applied written corporate policy or procedure.

450.2491a Definitions.
Sec. 491a.

As used in this section and sections 492a to 497:

(a) "Derivative proceeding" means a civil suit in the right of a domestic corporation or a foreign corporation that is authorized to or does conduct affairs in this state.

(b) "Director" includes an individual who was serving on the board of a corporation organized on a directorship basis at the time of the act or omission complained of and an individual who becomes a member of the board of that corporation after the act or omission.

(c) "Disinterested director" means an individual who is currently serving on the board of a corporation and is not a party to a derivative proceeding, or an individual who is currently serving on the board of a corporation and is a party to a derivative proceeding if the corporation demonstrates that the claim asserted against the director is frivolous or insubstantial.

(d) "Member" means a record or beneficial owner of a membership in a corporation that is organized on a membership basis and includes a beneficial owner whose membership is held in a voting trust or held by a nominee on the owner's behalf.

(e) "Shareholder" means a record or beneficial owner of shares of a corporation that is organized on a stock basis and includes a beneficial owner whose shares are held in a voting trust or held by a nominee on the owner's behalf.

450.2492a Derivate proceeding; criteria to be met by shareholder or member.
Sec. 492a.

A shareholder or member may not commence or maintain a derivative proceeding unless the shareholder or member meets all of the following criteria:

(a) The shareholder or member was a shareholder or member of the corporation at the time of the act or omission complained of or became a shareholder or member through a permitted transfer by operation of law from a person that was a shareholder or member at that time.

(b) The shareholder or member fairly and adequately represents the interests of the corporation in enforcing the right of the corporation.

(c) The shareholder or member continues to be a shareholder or member until the time of judgment, unless the failure to continue to be a shareholder or member is the result of corporate action in which the former shareholder or member did not acquiesce and the derivative proceeding was commenced before the termination of the former shareholder's or member's status as a shareholder or member.

450.2493a Derivative proceeding; commencement.
Sec. 493a.

A shareholder, member, or director may not commence a derivative proceeding until all of the following have occurred:

(a) A written demand is made on the corporation to take suitable action.

(b) Ninety days have expired from the date the demand was made unless the shareholder, member, or director is notified that the corporation has rejected the demand or unless irreparable injury to the corporation would result by waiting for the expiration of the 90-day period.

450.2494 Derivative proceeding; investigation; issuance of stay.
Sec. 494.

If the corporation commences an investigation of the allegations made in a demand under section 493 or a complaint in a derivative proceeding, the court may stay the derivative proceeding for a period that the court considers appropriate.

450.2495 Derivative proceeding; dismissal.
Sec. 495.

(1) On a motion by the corporation in a derivative proceeding, the court shall dismiss the proceeding if the court finds that 1 of the groups specified in subsection (2) has made a determination in good faith after conducting a reasonable investigation on which its conclusions are based, that the maintenance of the derivative proceeding is not in the best interests of the corporation. If the determination is made under subsection (2)(a) or (b), the corporation has the burden of proving the good faith of the group making the determination and the reasonableness of the investigation. If the determination is made under subsection (2)(c) or (d), the plaintiff has the burden of proving that the determination was not made in good faith or that the investigation was not reasonable.

(2) A determination under subsection (1) may be made by any 1 of the following:

(a) By a majority vote of the disinterested directors, if the disinterested directors constitute a quorum at a meeting of the board.

(b) By a majority vote of a committee that consists of 2 or more disinterested directors appointed by a majority vote of disinterested directors present at a meeting of the board, whether or not the disinterested directors constitute a quorum at the meeting.

(c) By a panel of 1 or more disinterested individuals who are appointed by the court on a motion by the corporation.

(d) By all disinterested directors.

450.2496 Derivative proceeding; discontinuance or settlement; court approval required.
Sec. 496.

A derivative proceeding shall not be discontinued or settled without the court's approval. If the court determines that a proposed discontinuance or settlement will substantially affect the interests of the corporation's shareholders or members or a class of shareholders or members, the court shall direct that notice be given to the shareholders or members affected and the court may determine whether 1 or more of the parties to the action shall bear the expense of giving the notice, in the amount as the court determines and finds to be reasonable under the circumstances. The court shall award the cost of the notice as special costs of the action, recoverable in the same manner as statutory taxable costs.

450.2497 Derivative proceeding; termination.
Sec. 497.

If a derivative proceeding is terminated, the court may order 1 of the following:
   (a) The plaintiff to pay any of the defendant's reasonable expenses, including reasonable attorney fees, incurred in defending the proceeding if it finds that the proceeding was commenced or maintained in bad faith or without reasonable cause.
   (b) The corporation to pay the plaintiff's reasonable expenses, including reasonable attorney fees, incurred in the proceeding if it finds that the proceeding has resulted in a substantial benefit to the corporation. The court shall direct the plaintiff to account to the corporation for any proceeds received by the plaintiff in excess of expenses awarded by the court, unless the judgment is rendered for the benefit of an injured shareholder or member only and limited to a recovery of the loss or damage sustained by the shareholder or member.

Chapter 5 – Board of Directors and Officers

450.2501 Board of directors; management of business and affairs of corporation; qualifications; powers.
Sec. 501.

(1) The business and affairs of a corporation shall be managed by or under the direction of its board, except as otherwise provided in this act or in its articles of incorporation. A director is not required to be a shareholder or member of the corporation unless the articles of incorporation or bylaws so require. The articles of incorporation or bylaws may prescribe qualifications for directors.
(2) The board of a corporation that is subject to the uniform prudent management of institutional funds act, 2009 PA 87, MCL 451.921 to 451.931, has the powers granted under both that act and this act. In the

event of an inconsistency between the 2 acts, the uniform prudent management of institutional funds act, 2009 PA 87, MCL 451.921 to 451.931, controls.

450.2501a Board of directors; minimum age; requirements.
Sec. 501a.

(1) A corporation organized for purposes described in section 501(c)(3) of the internal revenue code of 1986 may include 1 or more directors on its board who are 16 or 17 years of age as long as that number does not exceed 1/2 the total number of directors required for a quorum for the transaction of business.
(2) If a corporation described in subsection (1) may have more than 1 director who is 16 or 17 years of age, the corporation shall state in its articles of incorporation the number of directors who may be 16 or 17 years of age.

450.2505 Board; number, term, election or appointment, and resignation of directors.
Sec. 505.

(1) The bylaws shall fix the number of directors or establish the manner for fixing the number, unless the articles of incorporation fix the number, subject to the following:
  (a) The board of a private foundation and board of a corporation formed to provide care to a dentally underserved population under section 16625 of the public health code, 1978 PA 368, MCL 333.16625, shall consist of 1 or more directors.
  (b) The board of a corporation that is not described in subdivision (a) shall consist of 3 or more directors.
(2) The articles of incorporation or a bylaw adopted by the shareholders, members, or incorporators of a corporation that is organized on a stock or membership basis may specify the term of office and the manner of election or appointment of directors. If the articles of incorporation or bylaws do not specify the term of office or manner of election or appointment of directors, the first board of directors shall hold office until the first annual meeting of shareholders or members. At the first annual meeting of shareholders or members and at each subsequent annual meeting the shareholders or members shall elect directors to hold office until the succeeding annual meeting, except as provided in section 506.
(3) The articles of incorporation or a bylaw of a corporation that is organized on a directorship basis shall specify the term of office and the manner of election or appointment of directors.
(4) A director shall hold office for the term for which he or she is elected or appointed and until his or her successor is elected or appointed and qualified, or until his or her resignation or removal. A director may resign by written notice to the corporation. A resignation of a director is effective

when it is received by the corporation or at a later time if a later time is stated in the notice of resignation.

450.2506 Dividing directors up to 5 classes; election or appointment; term; expiration.
Sec. 506.

(1) The articles of incorporation or a bylaw adopted by the shareholders, members, or incorporators of a corporation that is organized on a stock or membership basis may provide that in lieu of annual election of all directors the directors are divided into up to 5 classes, each of which is as nearly equal in number as possible, and elected or appointed for the terms and in the manner as specified in the articles of incorporation or bylaws. If the articles of incorporation or the bylaws do not specify the term of office for the classes of directors, the term of office of directors in the first class shall expire at the first annual meeting of shareholders or members after their election, and that of each succeeding class shall expire at the next annual meeting after their election corresponding with the number of their class. At each annual meeting after classes are established, the shareholders or members shall elect a number of directors equal to the number of the class whose term expires at the time of the meeting to hold office until the next annual meeting corresponding with the number of their class.
(2) A corporation that has more than 1 class of shares or membership may provide in its articles of incorporation or a bylaw adopted by each class of shareholders or members for the election of 1 or more directors by shareholders or members of a class, to the exclusion of other shareholders or members.
(3) The articles of incorporation or bylaws of a corporation that is organized on a directorship basis may provide that the directors are divided into up to 5 classes, elected or appointed for the terms and in the manner as specified in the articles of incorporation or bylaws.

450.2511 Removal of director; vote.
Sec. 511.

(1) The shareholders or members of a corporation that is organized on a stock or membership basis may remove 1 or more directors with or without cause unless the articles of incorporation provide that directors may be removed only for cause. A vote of a majority of the shares or members entitled to vote at an election of directors is required for removal, except that the articles of incorporation may require a higher vote for removal without cause. This subsection does not invalidate any bylaw adopted before the effective date of the amendatory act that added this sentence to the extent that the bylaw applies to removal without cause.
(2) The directors of a corporation that is organized on a directorship basis may remove 1 or more directors with cause. The vote of a majority of the

directors then in office is required for a removal under this subsection. If authorized in the articles of incorporation or bylaws, a director of a corporation that is organized on a directorship basis who is appointed or elected by a person or persons other than the board of directors of the corporation may also be removed, with or without cause, by the person or persons that appointed or elected that director.

(3) If a corporation has cumulative voting, and less than the entire board is to be removed, no 1 of the directors may be removed if the votes cast against his or her removal are sufficient to elect him or her if cumulatively voted at an election of the entire board of directors, or, if there are classes of directors, at an election of the class of directors of which he or she is a part.

(4) If holders of a class of stock or of bonds or members of a class are entitled under the articles of incorporation or a bylaw adopted under section 506(2) to elect 1 or more directors, this section applies, with respect to removal of a director so elected, to the vote of the holders of the outstanding shares of that class of stock, the holders of those bonds, or the members of that class.

450.2514 Removal of director by circuit court.
Sec. 514.

(1) The circuit court for the county in which the principal place of business or registered office of a corporation is located may remove a director of the corporation from office in a proceeding commenced by the corporation, by its shareholders holding at least 10% of the outstanding shares of any class, or by 10% of the members if the court finds that the director engaged in fraudulent, illegal, or dishonest conduct or gross abuse of authority or discretion with respect to the corporation, and removal is in the best interest of the corporation.

(2) A court that removes a director under this section may bar him or her from serving as a director of the corporation for a period prescribed by the court.

(3) If shareholders or members commence a proceeding under subsection (1), they shall make the corporation a party defendant.

450.2515a Vacancy.
Sec. 515a.

(1) Unless otherwise limited in the articles of incorporation or bylaws, if a vacancy, including a vacancy resulting from an increase in the number of directors, occurs on a board, the corporation may fill the vacancy in any of the following manners:
  (a) The shareholders of a corporation that is organized on a stock basis or the members of a corporation that is organized on a membership basis may fill the vacancy.
  (b) The board may fill the vacancy.

    (c) If the directors remaining in office constitute fewer than a quorum of the board, they may fill the vacancy by the affirmative vote of a majority of all the directors remaining in office.

(2) Unless otherwise provided in the articles of incorporation or bylaws, if the holders of any class or classes of stock or the members of any class or classes are entitled to elect 1 or more directors to the exclusion of other shareholders or members, vacancies of that class or classes may be filled only by 1 of the following:

    (a) By a majority of the directors elected by the holders of that class or classes of stock or the members of that class or classes then in office, whether or not those directors constitute a quorum of the board.

    (b) By the holders of shares of that class or classes of shares or the members of that class or classes.

(3) Unless otherwise limited in the articles of incorporation or bylaws, if a corporation's directors are divided into classes, any director chosen to fill a vacancy shall hold office until the next election of the class for which the director was chosen, and until his or her successor is elected and qualified.

(4) If because of death, resignation, or other cause, a corporation has no directors in office, an officer, a shareholder, a member of a corporation that is organized on a membership basis, a personal representative, administrator, trustee, or guardian of a shareholder or member, or other fiduciary entrusted with the same responsibility for the person or estate of a shareholder or member, may call a special meeting of shareholders or members in accordance with the articles or the bylaws.

(5) A corporation may fill a vacancy that will occur at a specific date, by reason of a resignation that is effective at a later date under section 505 or otherwise, before the vacancy occurs, but a director who is elected or appointed under this subsection may not take office until the vacancy occurs.

450.2521 Regular or special meetings of board; location; notice; attendance or participation as waiver of notice; participation by means of conference telephone or other remote communication.
Sec. 521.

(1) A board may hold regular or special meetings of the board either in or outside of this state.

(2) A board may hold a regular meeting with or without notice as prescribed in the bylaws. A board may hold a special meeting after giving notice as prescribed in the bylaws. A director's attendance at or participation in a meeting waives any required notice to him or her of the meeting unless he or she at the beginning of the meeting, or when he or she arrives, objects to the meeting or the transacting of business at the meeting and after objecting does not vote for or assent to any action taken at the meeting. Unless required under the bylaws, notice or a waiver of notice of a meeting does not have to specify the business to be transacted or the purpose of, the regular or special meeting.

(3) Unless otherwise restricted in the articles of incorporation or bylaws, a member of the board or of a committee designated by the board may participate in a meeting by means of conference telephone or other means of remote communication if all individuals who are participating in the meeting can communicate with the other participants. Participation in a meeting under this subsection constitutes attendance in person at the meeting.

450.2523 Quorum; vote constituting action of board or committee; amendment of bylaws.
Sec. 523.

(1) A majority of the members of a board who are then in office, or of the members of a committee of the board, constitutes a quorum for the transaction of business, unless the articles of incorporation or bylaws, or in the case of a committee, the board resolution that establishes the committee, provide for a larger or smaller number. However, a quorum of the board may not be less than 1/3 of the members of the board who are then in office and a quorum of an executive committee acting on behalf of the board under section 527 may not be less than 1/3 of members of the executive committee. The vote of the majority of members present at a meeting at which a quorum is present constitutes the action of the board or of the committee, unless the vote of a larger number is required under this act, the articles of incorporation, or the bylaws, or in the case of a committee, the board resolution that establishes the committee.
(2) Amendment of the bylaws by a board requires the vote of not less than a majority of the members of the board then in office, unless the articles of incorporation or bylaws provide for a larger number.

450.2525 Taking action without meeting; consent.
Sec. 525.

Unless prohibited by the articles of incorporation or bylaws, action required or permitted to be taken under authorization voted at a meeting of the board or a committee of the board may be taken without a meeting if, before or after the action, all members of the board then in office or of the committee consent to the action in writing or by electronic transmission. The written consents shall be filed with the minutes of the proceedings of the board or committee. The consent has the same effect as a vote of the board or committee for all purposes.

450.2527 Designation of committees; membership; alternates; absent or disqualified member; providing for election or appointment of committees in articles or bylaws.
Sec. 527.

(1) Unless otherwise provided in the articles of incorporation or bylaws, the board may designate 1 or more executive committees, each executive committee to consist of 1 or more of the directors of the corporation. The board may designate 1 or more directors as alternate members of an executive committee, who may replace an absent or disqualified member at a meeting of the executive committee. The bylaws may provide that in the absence or disqualification of a member of an executive committee, the members present at a meeting and not disqualified from voting, whether or not they constitute a quorum, may unanimously appoint another member of the board to act at the meeting in place of the absent or disqualified member.

(2) An executive committee designated under subsection (1) and each member of an executive committee serves at the pleasure of the board.

(3) The articles of incorporation or bylaws may provide for the election or appointment of 1 or more executive committees that consist of 1 or more shareholders or members, 1 or more directors, or a combination of shareholders or members and directors.

(4) Unless otherwise prohibited in the articles of incorporation or bylaws, the board or an individual or individuals designated in the bylaws or by the board may appoint 1 or more committees that are not executive committees to assist in the conduct of its affairs and may provide of the creation of 1 or more subcommittees of any committee appointed under this subsection. The bylaws, or a resolution that establishes the committee and is approved by the board in the absence of a bylaw provision, shall state the purposes of the committees appointed under this subsection, the terms and qualifications of committee members, and the ways in which members of the committees are selected and removed. The board or authorized individuals may designate 1 or more individuals as alternate members of a committee appointed under this subsection who may replace an absent or disqualified committee member in a meeting of the committee. Some or all of the members of a committee appointed under this subsection may be individuals who are directors, officers, members, or shareholders of the corporation and some or all of the members of a committee appointed under this subsection may be individuals who are not directors, officers, members, or shareholders of the corporation, as provided in the bylaws or in the action or resolution or resolutions of the board that establish the committee. A committee that is appointed under this subsection is not an executive committee and may not execute the power or authority of the board in the management of the business and affairs of the corporation, but may perform under the direction of the board those functions described in the bylaws or determined from time to time by the board.

450.2528 Executive committee designated under MCL 450.2527(1) or (3); powers and authority; subcommittees.
Sec. 528.

(1) An executive committee that is designated under section 527(1) or (3), to the extent provided in the resolution of the board, in the articles of incorporation, or in the bylaws, may exercise any or all powers and authority of the board in management of the business and affairs of the corporation. An executive committee does not have power or authority to do any of the following:
   (a) Amend the articles of incorporation.
   (b) Adopt an agreement of merger or conversion.
   (c) Recommend to shareholders or members the sale, lease, or exchange of all or substantially all of the corporation's property and assets.
   (d) Recommend to shareholders or members a dissolution of the corporation or a revocation of a dissolution.
   (e) Amend the bylaws of the corporation.
   (f) Fill vacancies in the board.
   (g) Fix compensation of the directors for serving on the board or on a committee.
   (h) Cancel shares or terminate memberships.
(2) Unless the resolution, articles of incorporation, or bylaws expressly provide the power or authority, an executive committee does not have power or authority to declare a distribution authorized under section 301 or to authorize the issuance of shares or memberships.
(3) Unless otherwise provided in the resolution, articles of incorporation, or bylaws, an executive committee may create 1 or more subcommittees. Each subcommittee shall consist of 1 or more members of the committee. An executive committee or the board may delegate to a subcommittee any or all of the powers and authority of the committee.

450.2529 Submitting matter to vote.
Sec. 529.

A corporation may agree to submit a matter to a vote of its shareholders or members even if, after approving the matter, the board of directors later determines that it no longer recommends the matter or recommends against approval of the matter by the shareholders or members.

450.2531 Officers of corporation; membership; election or appointment; individual holding 2 or more offices; term of office; authority and duties.
Sec. 531.

(1) The officers of a corporation shall consist of a president, secretary, treasurer, and, if desired, a chairperson of the board, 1 or more vice presidents, and any other officers as prescribed in the bylaws or determined

by the board. Unless otherwise provided in the articles of incorporation or bylaws, the board shall elect or appoint the officers.

(2) One individual may hold 2 or more offices, but an officer shall not execute, acknowledge, or verify an instrument in more than 1 capacity if the instrument is required by law or the articles of incorporation or bylaws to be executed, acknowledged, or verified by 2 or more officers.

(3) An officer shall hold office for the term for which he or she is elected or appointed and until his or her successor is elected or appointed and qualified, or until his or her resignation or removal.

(4) An officer, as between himself or herself, other officers, and the corporation, has the authority and shall perform the duties in the management of the corporation provided in the bylaws, or determined in accordance with a resolution or resolutions of the board that is not inconsistent with the bylaws.

450.2535 Removal of officer; suspension of authority to act; contract rights; resignation of officer; notice.
Sec. 535.

(1) An officer elected or appointed by the board may be removed by the board with or without cause. An officer elected by the shareholders or members may be removed, with or without cause, only by vote of the shareholders or members. The authority of the officer to act as an officer may be suspended by the board for cause.

(2) The removal of an officer shall be without prejudice to the contract rights of the officer, if any. The election or appointment of an officer does not of itself create contract rights.

(3) An officer may resign by written notice to the corporation. The resignation is effective upon its receipt by the corporation or at a subsequent time specified in the notice of resignation.

450.2541 Director or officer; discharge of duties; manner; reliance on certain information; compliance; liability; claim for monetary damages for breach of volunteer director's duty; commencement of action.
Sec. 541.

(1) A director or officer shall discharge his or her duties as a director or officer including his or her duties as a member of a committee in the following manner:
   (a) In good faith.
   (b) With the care an ordinarily prudent person in a like position would exercise under similar circumstances.
   (c) In a manner he or she reasonably believes is in the best interests of the corporation.

(2) In discharging his or her duties, a director or officer is entitled to rely on information, opinions, reports, or statements, including financial statements and other financial data, if prepared or presented by any of the following:

   (a) One or more directors, officers, or employees of the corporation, or of a domestic or foreign corporation or a business organization under joint control or common control, whom the director or officer reasonably believes to be reliable and competent in the matters presented.

   (b) Legal counsel, public accountants, engineers, or other persons as to matters the director or officer reasonably believes are within the person's professional or expert competence.

   (c) A committee of the board of which he or she is not a member if the director or officer reasonably believes that the committee merits confidence.

(3) A director or officer is not entitled to rely on the information described in subsection (2) if he or she has knowledge concerning the matter in question that makes reliance otherwise permitted under subsection (2) unwarranted.

(4) A director or officer of a corporation that is subject to the uniform prudent management of institutional funds act, 2009 PA 87, MCL 451.921 to 451.931, is considered to be in compliance with this section if he or she complies with the uniform prudent management of institutional funds act, 2009 PA 87, MCL 451.921 to 451.931, in the administration of the powers specified in that act.

(5) If the corporation's articles of incorporation contain a provision authorized under section 209(1)(c), a director of the corporation is only personally liable for monetary damages for a breach of fiduciary duty as a director to the corporation, its shareholders, or its members to the extent set forth in the provision.

(6) If the corporation's articles of incorporation contain a provision authorized under section 209(1)(d), a claim for monetary damages for a breach of a volunteer director's duty to any person other than the corporation, its shareholders, or its members shall not be brought or maintained against the volunteer director. However, that claim may be brought or maintained against the corporation, and the corporation is liable for any breach of the volunteer director's duty.

(7) An action against a director or officer for failure to perform the duties imposed under this section shall be commenced within 3 years after the cause of action has accrued, or within 2 years after the time when the cause of action is discovered or should reasonably have been discovered, by the complainant, whichever occurs first.

450.2545a Transaction in which director or officer has interest.
Sec. 545a.

(1) A transaction in which a director or officer is determined to have an interest shall not be enjoined, set aside, or give rise to an award of damages or other sanctions because of the interest, in a proceeding by a shareholder, a member, or a director of a corporation that is organized on a directorship

basis or by or in the right of the corporation, if the person interested in the transaction establishes any of the following:

(a) The transaction was fair to the corporation at the time it was entered into.

(b) The material facts of the transaction and the director's or officer's interest were disclosed or known to the board or an executive committee of the board and the board or executive committee authorized, approved, or ratified the transaction.

(c) The material facts of the transaction and the director's or officer's interest were disclosed or known to the shareholders or members who are entitled to vote and they authorized, approved, or ratified the transaction.

(2) For purposes of subsection (1)(b), a transaction is authorized, approved, or ratified if it received the affirmative vote of the majority of the directors on the board or the executive committee who did not have an interest in the transaction, though less than a quorum. The presence of, or a vote cast by, a director with an interest in the transaction does not affect the validity of an action taken under subsection (1)(b).

(3) For purposes of subsection (1)(c), a transaction is authorized, approved, or ratified if it received the majority of votes that were cast by the holders of shares or members that did not have an interest in the transaction. A majority of the votes held by shareholders or members that did not have an interest in the transaction constitutes a quorum for the purpose of taking action under subsection (1)(c).

(4) Satisfying the requirements of subsection (1) does not preclude other claims relating to a transaction in which a director or officer is determined to have an interest. Those claims shall be evaluated under principles applicable to a transaction in which a director or officer does not have an interest.

(5) Unless the compensation is prohibited by the articles of incorporation or the bylaws, the board, by affirmative vote of a majority of directors in office and irrespective of any personal interest of any of them, may, subject to any limitations in the articles of incorporation or bylaws, establish reasonable compensation of directors for services to the corporation as directors or officers, but approval of the shareholders or members is required if the articles of incorporation, bylaws, or other provisions of this act require that approval. Transactions pertaining to the compensation of directors for services to the corporation as directors or officers shall not be enjoined, set aside, or give rise to an award of damages or other sanctions in a proceeding by a shareholder or member or by or in the right of the corporation unless it is shown that the compensation was unreasonable at the time it was established or exceeded amounts permitted under the articles of incorporation or bylaws.

450.2548 Loan, guaranty, or assistance by corporation for officer or employee.
Sec. 548.

(1) Unless otherwise prohibited by law or prohibited in the articles of incorporation or bylaws, a corporation may lend money to, guarantee an obligation of, or otherwise assist an officer or employee of the corporation or a subsidiary, including an officer or employee who is a director of the corporation or subsidiary, if in the judgment of the board, the loan, guaranty, or assistance is reasonably expected to benefit the corporation, or the loan, guaranty, or assistance is provided under a plan authorizing loans, guaranties, or assistance that the board has reasonably determined will benefit the corporation.

(2) A loan, guaranty, or assistance described in subsection (1) may be with or without interest, and may be unsecured, or secured in a manner that the board approves, including a pledge of shares of stock of a corporation that is organized on a stock basis or pledge of a membership in a corporation that is organized on a membership basis.

(3) This section does not deny, limit, or restrict the powers of guaranty or warranty of a corporation at common law or under any statute.

450.2551 Liability of directors for certain corporate actions; liability of shareholder or member accepting or receiving distribution contrary to act.
Sec. 551.

(1) Directors who vote for or concur in any of the following corporate actions are jointly and severally liable to the corporation for its benefit or for the benefit of its creditors, shareholders, or members, for any legally recoverable injury suffered by the corporation or those creditors, shareholders, or members as a result of the action in an amount that does not exceed the difference between the amount paid or distributed and the amount that lawfully could have been paid or distributed:
  (a) Declaring a share dividend or distribution to shareholders or members that is contrary to this act or contrary to any restriction in the articles of incorporation or bylaws.
  (b) Making a distribution to shareholders or members during or after dissolution of the corporation without paying or providing for debts, obligations, and liabilities of the corporation as required under section 855.
  (c) Making a loan to a director, officer, or employee of the corporation or a subsidiary of the corporation that is contrary to this act.

(2) A director is not liable under this section if he or she complies with section 541.

(3) A shareholder or member that accepts or receives a share dividend or distribution with knowledge of facts that indicate that it is contrary to this act, or any restriction in the articles of incorporation or bylaws, is liable to the corporation in the amount accepted or received in excess of the

shareholder's or member's share of the amount that the corporation could lawfully distribute.

450.2552 Rights of director against whom claim successfully asserted under MCL 450.2551.
Sec. 552.

(1) A director against whom a claim is successfully asserted under section 551 is entitled to contribution from the other directors who voted for, or concurred in, the action on which the claim is asserted.

(2) A director against whom a claim is successfully asserted under section 551 is entitled, to the extent of the amounts paid by him or her to the corporation as a result of the claims, to all of the following:

    (a) If the director pays the corporation any amount of an improper share dividend or distribution, to be subrogated to the rights of the corporation against shareholders or members that received the share dividend or distribution in proportion to the amounts received by them.

    (b) If the director pays the corporation any amount of the purchase price of an improper purchase of shares or memberships, to have the corporation rescind the purchase and recover for his or her benefit, but at his or her expense, the amount of the purchase price from any seller that sold the shares or memberships with knowledge of facts indicating that the purchase of shares or memberships by the corporation was not authorized by this act, or to have the corporation assign to the director any claim against the seller and, if consistent with its articles of incorporation and bylaws, the shares or memberships.

    (c) If the director pays the corporation the claim of a creditor because of a violation of section 551(1)(b), to be subrogated to the rights of the corporation against shareholders or members that received an improper distribution of assets.

    (d) If the director pays the corporation the amount of a loan made improperly to a director, officer, or employee, to be subrogated to the rights of the corporation against the director, officer, or employee who received the improper loan.

450.2553 Presence or absence of director at meeting at which action under MCL 450.2551 taken; presumption; dissent.
Sec. 553.

(1) If a director is present at a meeting of the board, or an executive committee of which he or she is a member, and action on a corporate matter described in section 551 is taken at that meeting, the director is presumed to concur in that action unless his or her dissent is entered in the minutes of the meeting or unless he or she files his or her written dissent to the action with the individual who is acting as secretary of the meeting before or promptly after

the adjournment of the meeting. The right to dissent does not apply to a director who voted in favor of the action.

(2) If a director who is absent from a meeting of the board, or an executive committee of which he or she is a member, and action on a corporate matter described in section 551 is taken at that meeting, the director is presumed to concur in the action unless he or she files his or her dissent with the secretary of the corporation within a reasonable time after he or she has knowledge of the action.

450.2554 Commencement of action under MCL 450.2551 or 450.2552.
Sec. 554.

An action against a director, shareholder, or member for recovery upon a liability imposed by section 551 shall be commenced within 3 years after the cause of action accrues. An action under section 552 shall be commenced within 3 years after payment by the director to the corporation.

450.2556 Volunteer's acts or omissions; claim for monetary damages.
Sec. 556.

If the corporation's articles of incorporation contain a provision authorized under section 209(e), then a claim for monetary damages for a volunteer director, volunteer officer, or other volunteer's acts or omissions shall not be brought or maintained against a volunteer director, volunteer officer, or other volunteer. The claim shall be brought and maintained against the corporation.

450.2561 Indemnification of director, officer, partner, trustee, employee, nondirector volunteer, or agent in connection with action, suit, or proceeding; conditions; presumption.
Sec. 561.

Unless otherwise provided by law or the articles of incorporation or bylaws of the corporation, a corporation has the power to indemnify a person that was or is a party or is threatened to be made a party to a threatened, pending, or completed action, suit, or proceeding, whether civil, criminal, administrative, or investigative and whether formal or informal, other than an action by or in the right of the corporation, by reason of the fact that the person is or was a director, officer, employee, nondirector volunteer, or agent of the corporation, or is or was serving at the request of the corporation as a director, officer, partner, trustee, employee, nondirector volunteer, or agent of another foreign or domestic corporation, business corporation, partnership, joint venture, trust, or other enterprise, whether for profit or not, for expenses, including attorneys' fees, judgments, penalties, fines, and amounts paid in settlement actually and reasonably incurred by the person in connection with the action, suit, or proceeding if the person acted in good faith and in a manner the person reasonably believed to be in or not opposed to the best interests of the corporation or its shareholders or members, and with respect to a criminal action or proceeding, if the person had no reasonable cause to believe that the conduct was unlawful. The termination of an action, suit, or proceeding by judgment, order, settlement, conviction, or upon a plea of nolo contendere or its equivalent, does not, of itself, create a presumption that the person did not act in good faith and in a manner that the person reasonably believed to be in or not opposed to the best interests of the corporation or its shareholders or members and, with respect to any criminal action or proceeding, had reasonable cause to believe that the conduct was unlawful.

450.2562 Indemnification against expenses of director, officer, partner, trustee, employee, nondirector volunteer, or agent in connection with action or suit by or in right of corporation; conditions; limitations.
Sec. 562.

Unless otherwise provided by law or in the articles of incorporation or bylaws of the corporation, a corporation has the power to indemnify a person that was or is a party or is threatened to be made a party to a threatened, pending, or completed action or suit by or in the right of the corporation to procure a judgment in its favor by reason of the fact that the person is or was a director, officer, employee, nondirector volunteer, or agent of the corporation, or is or was serving at the request of the corporation as a director, officer, partner, trustee, employee, nondirector volunteer, or agent of another foreign or domestic corporation, business corporation, partnership, joint venture, trust, or other enterprise, whether for profit or not, for expenses, including attorneys' fees and amounts paid in settlement actually and reasonably incurred by the person in connection with the action or suit if the person acted in good faith and in a manner the person reasonably believed to be in or not opposed to the best interests of the corporation or its shareholders or members. A corporation shall not indemnify a person for a claim, issue, or matter in which the person is found liable to the corporation except to the extent authorized under section 564c.

450.2563 Indemnification for expenses of director, officer, or nondirector volunteer successful in defense of action, suit, or proceeding referred to in MCL 450.2561 or 450.2562.
Sec. 563.

Unless otherwise provided by law or under the articles of incorporation or bylaws of the corporation, to the extent that a director, officer, or nondirector volunteer of a corporation is successful on the merits or otherwise in defense of an action, suit, or proceeding referred to in section 561 or 562, or in defense of a claim, issue, or matter in the action, suit, or proceeding, or has established that the corporation is required to assume the person's liabilities under section 209(1)(d) or (e), the corporation shall indemnify the person for actual and reasonable expenses, including attorneys' fees, incurred in connection with the action, suit, or proceeding and an action, suit, or proceeding brought to enforce the mandatory indemnification provided in this section.

450.2564a Indemnification of director, officer, employee, nondirector volunteer, or agent under MCL 450.2561 or 450.2562; authorization; basis; determination; evaluation; designation of committee or selection of legal counsel; indemnification for portion of expenses; payment; indemnification of director for expenses and liabilities.
Sec. 564a.

(1) Except as otherwise provided in subsection (5), unless ordered by the court, a corporation shall indemnify a director, officer, employee, nondirector volunteer, or agent under section 561 or 562, only if authorized in the specific case based on a determination that indemnification of the director, officer, employee, nondirector volunteer, or agent is proper in the circumstances because that person has met the applicable standard of conduct set forth in sections 561 and 562 and based on an evaluation that the expenses and amounts paid in settlement are reasonable. A corporation shall make a determination and evaluation under this subsection in 1 of the following ways:
   (a) By a majority vote of a quorum of the board that consists of directors who are not parties or threatened to be made parties to the action, suit, or proceeding.
   (b) If the board is unable to obtain a quorum under subdivision (a), by majority vote of a committee that is duly designated by the board and that consists solely of 2 or more directors who are not at the time parties or threatened to be made parties to the action, suit, or proceeding.
   (c) By independent legal counsel in a written opinion. The corporation must select counsel to prepare the opinion in 1 of the following ways:
      (i) By the board or a committee of directors in the manner described in subdivision (a) or (b).
      (ii) If the board is unable to obtain a quorum under subdivision (a) and the board is unable to designate a committee under subdivision (b), by the board.
   (d) By the shareholders or members, but shares or memberships held by directors, officers, employees, nondirector volunteers, or agents that are parties or threatened to be made parties to the action, suit, or proceeding may not be voted.
(2) All directors may participate in designating a committee under subsection (1)(b) or in selecting independent legal counsel under subsection (1)(c)(ii).
(3) If a person is entitled to indemnification under section 561 or 562 for a portion of expenses, including reasonable attorneys' fees, judgments, penalties, fines, and amounts paid in settlement, but not for the total amount, the corporation may indemnify the person for the portion of the expenses, judgments, penalties, fines, or amounts paid in settlement for which the person is entitled to be indemnified.

(4) A corporation shall authorize payment of indemnification under this section in any of the following ways:

   (a) By the board in 1 of the following ways:

      (i) If there are 2 or more directors who are not parties or threatened to be made parties to the action, suit, or proceeding, by a majority vote of all directors who are not parties or threatened to be made parties, a majority of whom shall constitute a quorum for this purpose.

      (ii) By a majority of the members of a committee of 2 or more directors who are not parties or threatened to be made parties to the action, suit, or proceeding.

      (iii) If there are fewer than 2 directors who are not parties or threatened to be made parties to the action, suit, or proceeding, by the vote necessary for action by the board under section 523. All directors may participate in authorization under this subparagraph.

   (b) By the shareholders or members, but shares or memberships held by directors, officers, employees, nondirector volunteers, or agents that are parties or threatened to be made parties to the action, suit, or proceeding may not be voted on the authorization.

(5) To the extent that the articles of incorporation eliminate or limit the liability of a director under section 209(1)(c), a corporation may indemnify a director for the expenses and liabilities described in this subsection without a determination that the director has met the standard of conduct set forth in sections 561 and 562, but shall not indemnify the director for obligations imposed under section 497(a) or, except to the extent authorized in section 564c, if the director received a financial benefit to which he or she was not entitled, intentionally inflicted harm on the corporation or its shareholders or members, violated section 551, or intentionally committed a criminal act. In connection with an action or suit by or in the right of the corporation described in section 562, indemnification under this subsection may be for expenses, including attorneys' fees, actually and reasonably incurred. In connection with an action, suit, or proceeding other than an action, suit, or proceeding by or in the right of the corporation, described in section 561, a corporation may indemnify a director under this subsection for expenses, including attorneys' fees, actually and reasonably incurred, and for judgments, penalties, fines, and amounts paid in settlement that are actually and reasonably incurred.

450.2564b Expenses incurred by director, officer, employee, nondirector volunteer, or agent; reimbursement; agreement; advances.
Sec. 564b.

(1) A corporation may pay or reimburse the reasonable expenses incurred by a director, officer, employee, nondirector volunteer, or agent of the corporation or a person that is or was serving at the request of the corporation as a director, officer, partner, trustee, employee, or agent of another domestic corporation, foreign corporation, domestic business

corporation, foreign business corporation, partnership, limited liability company, joint venture, trust, or other enterprise, whether for profit or not, that is a party or threatened to be made a party to an action, suit, or proceeding in advance of final disposition of the proceeding if the person furnishes the corporation a written agreement, executed personally or on the person's behalf, to repay the advance if it is ultimately determined that the person did not meet the standard of conduct, if any, required by this act for the indemnification of a person under the circumstances.

(2) An agreement required under subsection (1) must be an unlimited general obligation of the director, officer, employee, nondirector volunteer, or agent, but may be unsecured. A corporation may accept an agreement that is required under subsection (1) without reference to the financial ability of the person to make repayment.

(3) A corporation shall evaluate the reasonableness of advances under this section in the manner described in section 564a(1) for evaluating the reasonableness of expenses, and make an authorization in the manner described in section 564a(4) unless an advance is mandatory. A corporation may authorize advances with respect to a proceeding and determine the reasonableness of advances or approve a method for determining the reasonableness of advances in a single resolution covering the entire proceeding. However, unless the action or resolution provides otherwise, an authorizing or determining authority of the corporation may subsequently terminate or amend the authorization or determination with respect to advances that are not yet made.

(4) A provision in the articles of incorporation or bylaws, a resolution of the board or shareholders or members, or an agreement that makes indemnification mandatory shall also make the advancement of expenses mandatory unless the provision, resolution, or agreement specifically provides otherwise.

450.2564c Indemnification of director, officer, employee, nondirector volunteer, or agent; application to court; determination.
Sec. 564c.

A director, officer, employee, nondirector volunteer, or agent of the corporation that is a party or threatened to be made a party to an action, suit, or proceeding may apply for indemnification to the court that is conducting the proceeding or to another court of competent jurisdiction. After receiving an application, the court after giving any notice it considers necessary may order indemnification if it determines that all of the following are met:

(a) Indemnification is not prohibited under section 497(a) and is consistent with other applicable law and with any restrictions in the articles of incorporation or the bylaws.

(b) The person is fairly and reasonably entitled to indemnification in view of all the relevant circumstances, whether or not the person met the applicable standard of conduct set forth in section 561 or 562 or was adjudged liable as described in section 562. However, if the person is found liable, indemnification is limited to reasonable expenses incurred by the person.

450.2565 Indemnification or advance of expenses not exclusive of other rights; limitation; continuation; amended provision.
Sec. 565.

(1) An indemnification or advance of expenses provided under sections 561 to 564c is not exclusive of other rights to which a person seeking indemnification or advance of expenses may be entitled under the articles of incorporation, bylaws, or a contractual agreement. The total amount of expenses advanced or indemnified from all sources combined shall not exceed the amount of actual expenses incurred by the person that is seeking indemnification or advance of expenses.

(2) Indemnification under sections 561 to 565 continues for a person that ceases to be a director, officer, employee, nondirector volunteer, or agent and inures to the benefit of the heirs, personal representatives, and administrators of the person.

(3) A right of indemnification or to advancement of expenses under a provision of the articles of incorporation or the bylaws is not eliminated or impaired by an amendment to the provision after the occurrence of the act or omission that is the subject of the formal or informal, administrative or investigative action, suit, or proceeding for which indemnification or advancement of expenses is sought unless the provision in effect at the time of the act or omission explicitly authorizes that elimination or impairment after the action or omission has occurred.

450.2567 Purchase and maintenance of insurance on behalf of director, officer, employee, nondirector volunteer, or agent.
Sec. 567.

(1) A corporation may purchase and maintain insurance on behalf of any person that is or was a director, officer, employee, nondirector volunteer, or agent of the corporation, or that is or was serving at the request of the corporation as a director, officer, partner, trustee, employee, nondirector volunteer, or agent of another foreign or domestic corporation, foreign or domestic business corporation, limited liability company, partnership, joint venture, trust, or other enterprise for profit or nonprofit against any liability asserted against the person and incurred by the person in that capacity or arising out of the person's status as such, whether or not the corporation has the power to indemnify the person against liability under sections 561 to 565.

(2) If the articles of incorporation include a provision that eliminates or limits the liability of a director under section 209(1)(c), the corporation may purchase insurance on behalf of a director under subsection (1) from an insurer owned by the corporation, but insurance purchased from that insurer may insure a director against monetary liability to the corporation or its

shareholders or members only to the extent to which the corporation could indemnify the director under section 564a(5).

450.2569 Scope of "corporation" for purposes of MCL 450.2561 to 450.2567.
Sec. 569.

For purposes of sections 561 to 567, "corporation" includes all constituent corporations absorbed in a consolidation or merger, any corporation converted into another business entity, and the resulting or surviving foreign or domestic corporation, foreign or domestic business corporation or other business entity, so that a person that is or was a director, officer, employee, nondirector volunteer, or agent of the constituent corporation or is or was serving at the request of the constituent corporation as a director, officer, partner, trustee, employee, nondirector volunteer, or agent of another foreign or domestic corporation, foreign or domestic business corporation, partnership, limited liability company, joint venture, trust, or other profit or nonprofit enterprise shall stand in the same position under the provisions of this section with respect to the resulting or surviving corporation or business corporation as the person would if the person had served the resulting or surviving corporation, business corporation, or other business entity in the same capacity.

450.2571 Definitions.
Sec. 571.

As used in sections 561 to 567:
    (a) "Fines" includes any excise taxes assessed on a person with respect to an employee benefit plan.
    (b) "Other enterprises" includes employee benefit plans.
    (c) "Serving at the request of the corporation" includes any service as a director, officer, employee, nondirector volunteer, or agent of the corporation that imposes duties on, or involves services by, the director, officer, employee, nondirector volunteer, or agent with respect to an employee benefit plan, its participants, or its beneficiaries.
    (d) A person that acted in good faith and in a manner the person reasonably believed to be in the interest of the participants and beneficiaries of an employee benefit plan is considered to have acted in a manner "not opposed to the best interests of the corporation or its shareholders or members" as referred to in sections 561 and 562.

Chapter 6 – Amendment of Corporate Documents

450.2601 Amendment of articles of incorporation; contents.
Sec. 601.

(1) A corporation may amend its articles of incorporation if the amendment contains only provisions that original articles of incorporation filed at the time the amendment is made might lawfully contain.

(2) Subject to section 301(6), a corporation may amend its articles of incorporation to become a business corporation by adopting restated articles of incorporation under section 641 if the restated articles of incorporation contain only those provisions that original articles of incorporation of a business corporation formed under the business corporation act might contain. The adoption and filing of restated articles of incorporation under this subsection does not constitute a dissolution of the corporation.

(3) Subject to section 301(6), a corporation may amend its articles of incorporation to become a professional corporation by adopting restated articles of incorporation under section 641 if the restated articles of incorporation contain only those provisions that original articles of incorporation of a professional corporation formed under chapter 2A of the business corporation act, MCL 450.1281 to 450.1289, might contain. The adoption and filing of restated articles of incorporation under this subsection does not constitute a dissolution of the corporation.

450.2602 Amendment of articles of incorporation; purposes.
Sec. 602.

Without limiting the general power of amendment under section 601, a corporation may amend its articles of incorporation to do any of the following:

(a) Change its corporate name.

(b) Enlarge, limit, or otherwise change its corporate purposes or powers.

(c) Change the duration of the corporation.

(d) Increase or decrease the aggregate number of shares, or shares of any class that the corporation has authority to issue.

(e) Exchange, classify, reclassify, or cancel any of its issued or unissued shares.

(f) Change the designation of any of its issued or unissued shares, or change the qualifications, preferences, limitations, and relative rights of any of its issued or unissued shares or of its members.

(g) Change the issued or unissued shares of any class into a different number of shares of the same class or into the same or a different number of shares of other classes.

(h) Create new classes of shares or members that have rights and preferences superior to, inferior to, or equal with, the issued or unissued shares or the memberships of any class then authorized.

(i) Cancel or otherwise affect the right of the holders of the shares or memberships of any class to receive distributions which have accrued but have not been declared.

(j) Limit, deny, or grant to shareholders or members of a class the preemptive right to acquire shares or memberships of the corporation.

(k) Change its registered office or change its resident agent.

(l) Strike out, change, or add any provision for management of and conduct of the affairs of the corporation, or creating, defining, limiting, and regulating the powers of the corporation, its directors, shareholders, members, or any class of shareholders or members, including any provision that under this act is required or permitted to be set forth in the bylaws.

(m) Change its form of organization to a stock corporation or a nonstock corporation that is organized on a membership or directorship basis. An amendment under this subsection must comply with section 202(c) and (d) or section 202(e) and (f), as applicable.

450.2611 Amendment of articles by incorporation; amendment without shareholder or member action; manner of adoption; notice of meeting; vote on proposed amendment; requirements; adoption; number of amendments acted upon at 1 meeting; certificate of amendment.
Sec. 611.

(1) The articles of incorporation may be amended by either of the following:
   (a) Before the first meeting of the board, the incorporators by complying with section 631(1).
   (b) If the corporation is organized on a stock or membership basis and has not yet issued shares or memberships or accepted any written subscription for shares or memberships, the board of directors by complying with section 631(2).

(2) Unless the articles of incorporation provide otherwise, the board of a corporation that is organized on a stock or membership basis may adopt 1 or more of the following amendments to its articles of incorporation without shareholder or member action:
   (a) Extend the duration of the corporation if it was incorporated at a time when limited duration was required by law.
   (b) Delete the names and addresses of the initial directors.
   (c) Delete the name and address of a prior resident agent, if a statement of change is on file with the administrator.
   (d) Delete descriptions of the property of the corporation or its value.
   (e) Change each issued and unissued authorized share of an outstanding class into a greater number of whole shares if the corporation has only shares of that class outstanding.
   (f) Change the corporate name by adding, deleting, or changing the word "corporation", "incorporated", "company", "limited", "association", or "society" or the abbreviation "corp.", "inc.", "co.", "ltd.", or "assn.", or

a similar word or abbreviation in the corporate name, or by adding, deleting, or changing a geographical attribution for the corporate name.

(g) Any other change that is expressly permitted under this act to be made without shareholder or member approval.

(3) Except for an amendment described in subsections (1) and (2) and except as otherwise provided in this act, a corporation must adopt any amendment to the articles of incorporation in 1 of the following manners:

(a) If the corporation is organized on a membership basis, by a vote of the members that are entitled to vote on the amendment.

(b) If the corporation is organized on a stock basis, by a vote of the shareholders that are entitled to vote on the amendment.

(c) If the corporation is organized on a directorship basis, unless the articles of incorporation specify a different manner, by a vote of the directors.

(4) A corporation or a member, shareholder, or director that proposes an amendment to the articles of incorporation shall give notice of a meeting to consider an amendment to the articles of incorporation to each member, shareholder, or director that is entitled to vote on the amendment, as applicable. The notice shall contain the proposed amendment or a summary of the changes that will occur if the amendment is adopted. The corporation or a member, shareholder, or director that proposes an amendment to the articles of incorporation shall provide the notice within the time and in the manner provided in this act for giving notice of meetings of shareholders, members, or directors, except that, in the case of a corporation that is organized on a directorship basis, the notice of the meeting shall be given to each director who is then in office at least 10 days before the meeting.

(5) At a meeting to consider an amendment to the articles of incorporation, a vote of shareholders, members, or directors entitled to vote shall be taken on the proposed amendment. The proposed amendment is approved if a majority of the votes that are held by shareholders or members entitled to vote on the proposed amendment are cast in favor of the amendment or, in the case of a corporation that is organized on a directorship basis, if it receives the affirmative vote of a majority of the directors then in office. If any class of shares or members is entitled to vote on the proposed amendment as a class, a majority of the votes that are held by shareholders or members of that class must also be cast in favor of the amendment to approve it. The voting requirements of this section are subject to any greater requirements under this act for specific amendments, or as provided in the articles of incorporation or bylaws. In addition, unless a greater vote is required in the articles of incorporation, or in a bylaw adopted by the shareholders, members, or directors of a corporation that is organized on a directorship basis, the proposed amendment is approved if a majority of the votes cast by members or shareholders present in person, by proxy, or by electronic transmission at the meeting are cast in favor of the amendment and, if any class of shares or members is entitled to vote on the proposed amendment as a class, a majority of the votes held by shareholders or members of each of those classes that are present in person, by proxy, or by

electronic transmission at the meeting are cast in favor of the amendment, or a majority of a quorum of the board of directors of a corporation that is organized on a directorship basis vote in favor of the amendment, if due notice of the time, place, and object of the meeting was given by mail, at the last known address, to each shareholder, member, or director entitled to vote at least 20 days before the date of the meeting or by publication in a publication distributed by the corporation to its shareholders or members at least 20 days before the date of the meeting.

(6) The shareholders, members, or directors may act on any number of amendments at 1 meeting.

(7) If an amendment to the articles of incorporation is adopted, the corporation shall file a certificate of amendment as provided in section 631.

450.2615 Voting as class on proposed amendment.
Sec. 615.

(1) The holders of a class of outstanding shares of a corporation that is organized on a stock basis or the members of a class of a corporation that is organized on a membership basis may vote as a class on a proposed amendment, whether or not entitled to vote on the amendment under the articles of incorporation, if the amendment would increase or decrease the aggregate number of authorized shares of the class or alter or change the powers, preferences, or special rights of the shares or members of the class or other classes so as to affect the class adversely.

(2) This section does not confer voting rights on members of a corporation that is organized on a directorship basis.

450.2631 Certificate of amendment; signing and execution; filing; contents.
Sec. 631.

(1) If an amendment to the articles of incorporation is approved under section 611(1)(a), a majority of the incorporators shall sign and file a certificate of amendment on behalf of the corporation that sets forth the amendment and certifies that the amendment was adopted by unanimous consent of the incorporators before the first meeting of the board.

(2) If an amendment to the articles of incorporation is approved under section 611(1)(a) or section 611(2), an officer of the corporation shall execute and file a certificate of amendment on behalf of the corporation that sets forth the amendment and certifies that it was adopted by the board of directors.

(3) Except for an amendment to the articles of incorporation described in subsection (1) or (2) or as otherwise provided in this act, if an amendment is approved, an officer of the corporation shall execute and file a certificate of amendment on behalf of the corporation that sets forth the amendment and certifies that the amendment was adopted in the manner required under section 611(3).

(4) If a corporation amends an article in its articles of incorporation that is divided into separately identified sections, the certificate of amendment may only set forth the section of the article that was amended. Otherwise, the certificate of amendment must set forth the entire article that was amended.

450.2641 Integrating provisions of articles into single instrument; adoption of restated articles of incorporation; adoption before first meeting; amendments subject to other provisions of act.
Sec. 641.

(1) A corporation may integrate into a single instrument the provisions of its articles of incorporation that are then in effect and operative, as amended, and at the same time may also further amend its articles of incorporation by adopting restated articles of incorporation.
(2) All of the incorporators may adopt restated articles of incorporation before the first meeting of the board by complying with sections 611(1)(a), 642, and 643(1).
(3) Other restated articles of incorporation shall be approved as follows:
  (a) If the restated articles of incorporation merely restate and integrate, but do not further amend the articles of incorporation as previously amended, the board may adopt the restated articles of incorporation without a vote of the shareholders or members, or the shareholders or members may adopt them, in which case the procedure and vote required under section 611(3) are applicable.
  (b) If the restated articles of incorporation restate, integrate, and also further amend the articles of incorporation, but those amendments include only amendments adopted under section 611(1)(b) or (2), the board may adopt the restated articles of incorporation without a vote of the shareholders or members.
  (c) If the restated articles of incorporation restate and integrate and also further amend in any material respect the articles of incorporation, as previously amended, in a way that is not previously addressed under this section, a vote of the shareholders, members, or directors under section 611(3) is required to adopt restated articles of incorporation.
(4) An amendment that is adopted in connection with the restatement of the articles of incorporation is subject to any other provision of this act, not inconsistent with this section, that would apply if a certificate of amendment were filed to effect that amendment.

450.2642 Restated articles of incorporation; heading or introductory paragraph; designation; required statements; omitted provisions.
Sec. 642.

(1) The heading of restated articles of incorporation shall specifically designate them as such. They shall state, either in the heading or in an introductory

paragraph, the corporation's present name, and, if it has been changed, all of its former names and the date of filing of its original articles of incorporation. Restated articles of incorporation shall state that they were duly adopted by the incorporators, directors, shareholders, or members under section 641.

(2) If adopted by the incorporators under section 641(2), restated articles of incorporation shall state that they were duly adopted by unanimous consent of the incorporators before the first meeting of the board under section 611(1)(a). If adopted by the board without a vote of the shareholders or members according to the procedure and vote required under section 641(3), the restated articles of incorporation shall state all of the following:

(a) That they only restate and integrate and do not further amend the existing articles as previously amended, or that the restated articles of incorporation only restate and integrate the articles and include only amendments adopted under section 611(1) or section 611(2).

(b) That there is no material discrepancy between those provisions and the provisions of the restated articles of incorporation.

(3) Restated articles of incorporation may omit any provisions of the original, amended, or previously restated articles of incorporation that named the incorporators, the initial board, or original subscribers for shares or original members or describe or value corporate property, and the omission is not considered a further amendment.

450.2643 Restated articles of incorporation; signing, filing, and executing; effect.
Sec. 643.

(1) A majority of incorporators shall sign and file restated articles of incorporation adopted under section 641(3) as provided in section 131.

(2) Except as provided in subsection (1), a corporation shall execute and file restated articles of incorporation as provided in section 131.

(3) When a filing of restated articles of incorporation becomes effective, the corporation's original articles of incorporation and previous amendments are superseded, and the restated articles of incorporation, including any amendments that are included in the restated articles of incorporation, are the articles of incorporation of the corporation.

450.2651 Abandonment of amendment; certificate.
Sec. 651.

Before the effective date of an amendment to the articles of incorporation for which shareholder, member, or director approval is required by this act, the amendment may be abandoned pursuant to provisions therefor, if any, set forth in the resolution of the shareholders, members, or directors approving the amendment. If a certificate of amendment has been filed by the corporation, it shall file a certificate of abandonment, but not later than the proposed effective date within 10 days after the abandonment.

Chapter 7 – Merger and Conversion

450.2701 Merger of domestic corporations; plan; contents; distributions.
Sec. 701.

(1) Two or more domestic corporations may merge into 1 of the corporations pursuant to a plan of merger approved in the manner provided in this act.
(2) The board of each corporation that proposes to participate in a merger shall adopt a plan of merger that contains all of the following:
    (a) The name of each constituent corporation and the name of the constituent corporation that will be the surviving corporation.
    (b) For each constituent corporation that is a stock corporation, the designation and number of outstanding shares of each class, specifying the classes that are entitled to vote; each class that is entitled to vote as a class; and, if the number of shares is subject to change before the effective date of the merger, the manner in which the change may occur.
    (c) For each constituent corporation that is a membership corporation, a description of the members, including the number, classification, and voting rights of members.
    (d) For each constituent corporation that is a directorship corporation, a description of the organization of the board, including the number, classification, and voting rights of directors.
    (e) The terms and conditions of the proposed merger, including the manner and basis of converting the shares of or membership or other interest in each constituent corporation into shares, obligations, or other securities of or membership or other interest in the surviving corporation, or into cash or other consideration, if any, that may include shares, bonds, rights, or other property or securities of or membership or other interests in a corporation whether or not a party to the merger, or into a combination of those securities, interests, and property.
    (f) A statement of any amendment to the articles of incorporation of the surviving corporation to result from the merger or any restatement of the articles of incorporation under section 641(1), in the form for restated articles of incorporation required under section 642.
    (g) Other provisions with respect to the proposed merger that the board considers necessary or desirable.
(3) Notwithstanding the provisions of this section and other provisions of this act, a corporation shall make distributions to shareholders or members of any corporation or to any other person in connection with a merger only in conformity with section 301 and with limitations on distributions in the articles of incorporation of that corporation.

450.2703a Plan of merger; approval.
Sec. 703a.

(1) Except as provided in subsection (2)(e) and (f), a plan of merger adopted by the board of each constituent corporation that is organized on a stock or membership basis shall, except as provided in subsection (2)(e) and (f), be submitted for approval at a meeting of the shareholders or members.

(2) For approval of a plan of merger under subsection (1), all of the following apply:

    (a) The board must recommend the plan of merger to the shareholders or members, unless section 529 applies or the board determines that because of conflict of interest, events that occur after the board adopts the plan, contractual obligations, or other special circumstances it should make no recommendation. If 1 or more of the exceptions described in this subdivision apply, the board must communicate the basis for not making a recommendation to the shareholders or members.

    (b) The board may condition its submission of the proposed merger on any basis.

    (c) Except as provided in subdivision (h), the corporation shall give notice of the shareholder or membership meeting to each shareholder or member of record, whether or not entitled to vote at the meeting, within the time and in the manner provided in this act for giving notice of meetings of shareholders or members. The notice shall include or be accompanied by a copy or summary of the plan of merger. If a summary of the plan is given, the notice shall state that a copy of the plan is available on request.

    (d) At the meeting of the shareholders or members, the shareholders or members shall vote on the proposed plan of merger. Subject to subdivision (e), the plan is approved if all of the following are met:

        (i) A majority of the votes held by shareholders or members of the corporation that are entitled to vote on the plan are cast in favor of the plan.

        (ii) If a class of members or shareholders is entitled to vote on the plan as a class, a majority of the votes held by shareholders or members of the class are cast in favor of the plan. A class of shares or of members is entitled to vote as a class in the case of a merger if the plan of merger contains a provision that, if contained in a proposed amendment to the articles of incorporation, would entitle the class of shares or members to vote as a class.

    (e) Notwithstanding subdivision (d), unless a greater vote is required in the articles of incorporation or in a bylaw adopted by the shareholders or members, if there are more than 20 shareholders or members that are entitled to vote at the meeting, the plan of merger is adopted if a majority of the votes held by shareholders or the members present in person or by proxy at the meeting are cast in favor of the plan and, if a class of shareholders or members is entitled to vote on the proposed merger as a class, a majority of the votes held by shareholders or members of that class present in person or by proxy at the meeting are cast in favor of the plan.

(f) Except as provided in section 754 or unless required in the articles of incorporation or bylaws, action on a plan of merger by the shareholders or members of a surviving corporation that is organized on a stock or membership basis is not required if all of the following apply:

    (i) The articles of incorporation of the surviving corporation will not differ from its articles of incorporation before the merger.

    (ii) Each shareholder of the surviving corporation whose shares were outstanding immediately before the effective date of the merger will hold the same number of shares, with identical designations, voting rights, preferences, limitations, and relative rights, immediately after the merger or each member of the surviving corporation whose membership was outstanding immediately before the effective date of the merger will be a member with identical designations, voting rights, preferences, limitations, and relative rights, immediately after the merger.

(g) A plan of merger may provide for differing forms of consideration for holders of shares or memberships within the same class based on the election of the holders or members, the amount of shares or memberships held, or another reasonable basis.

(h) A corporation that has more than 20 shareholders or members is not required to give notice under subdivision (c) to any shareholder or member, and is not required to allow the shareholder or member to vote on a proposed plan of merger or conversion, if both of the following apply:

    (i) The shareholder or member is not entitled to vote on the proposed plan of merger or conversion under the articles of incorporation or bylaws of the corporation.

        (i) The shareholder or member is not entitled to receive any distributions from the corporation on dissolution under the articles of incorporation or bylaws of the corporation, under this act, or under other applicable law.

(3) If any merging corporation is organized on a directorship basis, the board shall approve a plan of merger by an affirmative vote of a majority of the directors who are then in office or a higher number of directors if specified in the articles of incorporation or bylaws. The corporation shall give notice of the meeting to authorize the merger to each director who is then in office at least 20 days before the meeting. The notice shall include or be accompanied by a copy or a summary of the plan of merger.

(4) If a person solicits proxies in connection with the approval of a plan of merger under this section from more than 25 shareholders or members, the person soliciting the proxies must provide a form of proxy to each voting shareholder or member solicited that contains all of the following:

    (a) A blank space for the date and the signature of a shareholder or member that is voting by proxy.

(b) Clear identification of each matter or group of related matters on which the shareholders or members are voting.

(c) The phrase "revocable proxy".

(d) An acknowledgment that the shareholder or member received the notice of meeting and the plan or a summary of the plan of merger.

(e) The date, time, and place of the meeting of the shareholders or members.

(f) A place for the shareholder or member to indicate on the proxy whether the shareholder or member votes for, votes against, or abstains from voting on the merger.

(g) A statement that the person designated as the proxy holder will vote the proxy in accordance with the instructions of the shareholder or member.

(h) A statement indicating how the proxy holder will vote the proxy if the shareholder or member does not specify a choice for a matter.

(i) A statement that if the proxy is not returned by the shareholder or member, the proxy holder may vote any valid proxy previously executed by the shareholder or member.

450.2706 Merger of domestic corporation with domestic or foreign corporation; conditions; consent; execution of certificate of merger; participation of other corporations.
Sec. 706.

(1) If a domestic corporation has not commenced business, has not issued any shares or memberships, and has not elected a board, the corporation may merge with any domestic or foreign corporation by unanimous consent of its incorporators.

(2) If incorporators unanimously consent to a merger under subsection (1), a majority of incorporators shall execute a certificate of merger under section 707.

(3) The other domestic or foreign corporations that participate in the merger with a domestic corporation under subsection (1) shall comply with the provisions of this act dealing with mergers that are applicable to them.

450.2707 Certificate of merger; signing and filing; contents; determining effectiveness.
Sec. 707.

(1) After a plan of merger is approved under this act, each constituent corporation shall sign and file a certificate of merger on behalf of that corporation. The certificate shall set forth all of the following:
   (a) The statements required under section 701(2)(a), (b), and (d), and the manner and basis of converting the shares or memberships of each constituent corporation that is organized on a stock or membership basis as set forth in the plan of merger.

   (b) A statement that the boards have adopted the plan of merger under section 701.

   (c) A statement that the surviving corporation will furnish the plan of merger, on request and without cost, to any shareholder or member of any constituent corporation.

   (d) If approval of the shareholders or members of 1 or more corporations that are parties to the merger was required, a statement that the plan was approved by the shareholders or members under section 703a.

   (e) If section 706 applies to the merger, a statement that the merging corporation has not commenced business, has not issued any shares or memberships, and has not elected a board and that the plan of merger was approved by the unanimous consent of the incorporators.

   (f) A statement of any assumed names of merging corporations that are transferred to the surviving corporation under section 217(3), specifying each transferred assumed name and the name of the corporation from which it is transferred. The certificate may include a statement of corporate names or assumed names of merging corporations that are to be treated as newly filed assumed names of the surviving corporation under section 217(4).

(2) Section 131 applies in determining when a certificate of merger under this section becomes effective.

450.2711 Merger of domestic corporation with subsidiary corporation; approval of plan of merger; mailing copy of plan to minority shareholder or member of record; other provisions; definitions.
Sec. 711.

(1) A domestic corporation may merge 1 or more subsidiary corporations into itself, or may merge itself, or itself and any 1 or more subsidiary corporations, into any other subsidiary corporation, without approval of the shareholders or members of any of the corporations, except as provided in section 713. The board of the parent corporation shall approve a plan of merger that sets forth those matters required to be set forth in a plan of merger under section 701. Approval by the board of a subsidiary corporation described in this subsection is not required.

(2) If the parent corporation owns less than 100% of the outstanding shares or memberships of any subsidiary corporation that is a constituent corporation, the parent corporation shall promptly after the filing of the certificate of merger mail a copy or summary of the plan of merger to each minority shareholder or member of record of each subsidiary corporation, unless the shareholder or member waives the requirement in writing or unless the subsidiary corporation is required to obtain the approval of its shareholders or members under section 713.

(3) The authority of a corporation to merge under this section does not prevent the corporation from using other provisions of this act to complete a merger.

(4) As used in this section and in sections 712 and 713:

(a) "Constituent corporation" means a corporation that is a party to the merger described in subsection (1).

(b) A domestic corporation is a "subsidiary corporation" if another domestic corporation holds at least 90% of its shareholder or member votes.

450.2712 Certificate of merger; execution and filing of certificate of merger by parent company; determination of effective date.
Sec. 712.

(1) After a plan of merger is adopted under section 711, the parent corporation shall execute and file a certificate of merger that sets forth all of the following:

(a) The statements required under section 701(2)(a) and (d), and the manner and basis of converting shares or memberships of each constituent corporation as set forth in the plan of merger.

(b) The number of outstanding shares or memberships of each class of each subsidiary corporation that is a party to the merger and the number of shares or memberships of each class owned by the parent corporation.

(c) A statement of any assumed names of merging corporations transferred to the surviving corporation as under section 217(3), specifying each transferred assumed name and the name of the corporation from which it is transferred. The certificate may include a statement of corporate names or assumed names of merging corporations that are to be treated as newly filed assumed names of the surviving corporation under section 217(4).

(2) Section 131 applies in determining when a certificate of merger becomes effective under this section.

450.2713 Subsidiary corporation as constituent corporation in merger; approval of shareholders or members.
Sec. 713.

(1) A subsidiary corporation that is a constituent corporation in a merger under section 711 shall obtain the approval of its shareholders or members in accordance with the applicable provisions of section 703a.

(2) A parent corporation shall obtain approval of its shareholders or members for a merger under section 711 if either of the following applies:

(a) Its articles of incorporation require shareholder or member approval of the merger.

(b) Pursuant to section 703a, the plan of merger contains a provision that would amend any part of the articles of incorporation of the parent corporation into which a subsidiary corporation is being merged, or a subsidiary corporation is to be the surviving corporation of the merger.

450.2724 Merger other than under MCL 450.2736a.
Sec. 724.

All of the following apply when a merger, other than a merger under section 736a, takes effect:

    (a) Every other corporation that is a party to the merger merges into the surviving corporation and the separate existence of every corporation that is a party to the merger except the surviving corporation ceases. A merger in which a domestic corporation is the surviving corporation is not considered a dissolution of any constituent domestic corporation or domestic business corporation.

    (b) The title to all real estate and other property and rights owned by each corporation that is a party to the merger is vested in the surviving corporation without reversion or impairment.

    (c) The surviving corporation may use the corporate name and the assumed names of any merging corporation, if the filings required under section 217(3) and (4) are made.

    (d) The surviving corporation has all of the liabilities of each corporation that is a party to the merger.

    (e) A person may continue any proceeding that is pending against any corporation that is a party to the merger as if the merger did not occur or the surviving corporation may be substituted in the proceeding for the corporation whose existence ceased.

    (f) The articles of incorporation of the surviving corporation are amended to the extent provided in the plan of merger.

    (g) The shares or memberships of each corporation party to the merger that are to be converted into shares, obligations, or other securities of or membership or other interests in the surviving or any other corporation or into cash or other property are converted.

450.2735 Merger of domestic business corporation, foreign corporation, or foreign business corporation with domestic corporation; surviving corporation; compliance; liability for enforcement of obligation; acquisition of shares or memberships through voluntary exchange; distributions.
Sec. 735.

    (1) One or more domestic business corporations, foreign corporations, or foreign business corporations may merge with 1 or more domestic corporations if all of the following are met:

        (a) In a merger involving a foreign corporation or a foreign business corporation, the merger is permitted under the law of the state or country under whose law each foreign corporation and each foreign business corporation is incorporated and each foreign corporation or foreign business corporation complies with that law in effecting the merger. If the parent corporation in a merger conducted under section 711 is a foreign corporation or a foreign business corporation, it shall comply with all of the following, notwithstanding the provisions of the laws of its jurisdiction of incorporation:

    (i)   Section 711(2) with respect to notice to shareholders or members of a domestic subsidiary corporation that is a party to the merger.

    (ii) Section 712 with respect to the certificate of merger.

  (b) If a foreign corporation that is authorized to conduct affairs or transact business in this state is a party to the merger, it shall comply with the applicable provision of sections 1021 and 1035.

  (c) In a merger involving 1 or more domestic business corporations, the merger is permitted under the business corporation act, and each domestic business corporation complies with that law in effecting the merger. However, if the parent corporation in a merger that is conducted under section 711 is a domestic business corporation, it shall also comply with all of the following:

    (i)   Section 711(2) with respect to notice to shareholders or members of a domestic subsidiary corporation that is a party to the merger.

    (ii) Section 712 with respect to the certificate of merger.

  (d) Each domestic corporation complies with the applicable provisions of sections 701 to 713.

(2) If the surviving corporation of a merger is a foreign corporation to be governed by the laws of a jurisdiction other than this state, it shall comply with the provisions of this act with respect to foreign corporations if it is to conduct affairs in this state. If the surviving corporation in a merger is a foreign business corporation to be governed by the laws of a jurisdiction other than this state, it shall comply with the provisions of the business corporation act with respect to foreign business corporations if it is to transact business in this state.

(3) The surviving corporation in a merger is liable, and is subject to service of process in a proceeding in this state, for the enforcement of an obligation of a domestic corporation that is party to the merger.

(4) This section does not limit the power of a domestic business corporation, foreign corporation, or foreign business corporation to acquire all or part of the shares or memberships of 1 or more classes of a domestic corporation through a voluntary exchange or otherwise.

(5) Notwithstanding this section or any other provisions of this act, a corporation shall make distributions to its shareholders or members or to any other person in connection with a merger with a domestic business corporation, foreign corporation, or foreign business corporation under this section only in conformity with section 301 and with any limitations on distributions in the articles of the corporation.

450.2736a Merger of domestic corporations with business organizations; requirements; merger of domestic corporation with domestic or foreign entity; consent; executing and filing certificate of merger; contents; effect of

merger; surviving entity; liability for enforcement of obligation; distributions; applicability of MCL 450.2735; definitions.
Sec. 736a.

(1) Except as provided in subsection (2) and subject to subsection (8), 1 or more domestic corporations may merge with 1 or more business organizations if all of the following requirements are met:

  (a) The merger is permitted under the law of the jurisdiction in which each constituent business organization is organized and each constituent business organization complies with that law in effecting the merger, and each foreign constituent business organization transacting business in this state complies with the applicable laws of this state.

  (b) The board of each domestic corporation that is participating in the merger adopts a plan of merger that sets forth all of the following:

    (i) The name of each constituent entity, the name of the constituent entity that will be the surviving entity, the street address of the surviving entity's principal place of business, and the type of organization of the surviving entity.

    (ii) If a domestic corporation that is a party to the merger is a stock corporation, the designation and number of outstanding shares of each class, specifying the classes entitled to vote, each class entitled to vote as a class, and, if the number of shares is subject to change before the effective date of the merger, the manner in which the change may occur.

    (iii) If a domestic corporation that is a party to the merger is a membership corporation, a description of the members, including the number, classification, and voting rights of members.

    (iv) If a domestic corporation that is a party to a merger is a directorship corporation, a description of the organization of the board, including the number, classification, and voting rights of directors.

    (v) The terms and conditions of the proposed merger, including the manner and basis of converting the shares, partnership interests, membership interests, or other ownership interests of each constituent entity into ownership interests, obligations, or other securities of or membership or other interests in the surviving entity, or into cash or other consideration, if any, that may include ownership interests, obligations, or other securities of or membership or other interests in an entity that is not a party to the merger, or into a combination of those securities, interests, or property.

    (vi) If the surviving entity is to be a domestic corporation, a statement of any amendment to the articles of incorporation of the surviving corporation that will result from the merger or any restatement of the articles under section 641(1), in the form for restated articles required under section 642.

      (vii) Any other provisions with respect to the proposed merger that the board considers necessary or desirable.

    (c) A plan of merger adopted by the board of each constituent domestic corporation shall be submitted for approval at a meeting of the shareholders or members under section 703a(1) or, if the corporation is organized on a directorship basis, for approval by the board of directors under section 703a(3).

(2) If a domestic corporation has not commenced business, has not issued any shares, and has not elected a board, the corporation may merge with any domestic or foreign entity by unanimous consent of its incorporators. If the incorporators unanimously consent to a merger under this subsection, a majority of the incorporators must execute and file a certificate of merger under subsection (3).

(3) After a plan of merger is approved under subsection (1) or the merger is approved under subsection (2), each domestic corporation that is a party to the merger shall execute and file a certificate of merger. The certificate shall set forth all of the following:

    (a) A statement of the applicable requirements set forth in subsection (1)(b)(i), (ii), (iii), (iv), (v), (vi), and (vii), and the manner and basis of converting the ownership, membership, or other interests of each constituent entity included in the plan of merger.

    (b) A statement that the plan of merger has been adopted by the board under subsection (1)(b).

    (c) A statement that the surviving entity will furnish the plan of merger, on request and without cost, to any shareholder or member of the domestic corporation.

    (d) If approval of the shareholders or members of the domestic corporation is required, a statement that the plan was approved by the shareholders or members under subsection (1)(c) or, if the corporation is organized on a directorship basis, a statement that the plan was approved by the board of directors under subsection (1)(c).

    (e) If subsection (2) applies to the merger, a statement that the corporation has not commenced business, has not issued any shares or memberships, and has not elected a board, and that the merger was approved by the unanimous consent of the incorporators.

    (f) A statement of any assumed names of merging entities that are transferred to the surviving entity under section 217(3), specifying each transferred assumed name and the name of the entity from which it is transferred. If the surviving entity is a domestic corporation or a foreign corporation authorized to conduct affairs in this state, the certificate may include a statement of the names or assumed names of merging entities that are to be treated as newly filed assumed names of the surviving corporation under section 217(4).

(4) Section 131 applies in determining when a certificate of merger under subsection (3) becomes effective.

(5) When a merger under this section takes effect, all of the following apply:

(a) Every other entity that is a party to the merger merges into the surviving entity and the separate existence of every entity that is a party to the merger except the surviving entity ceases.

(b) The title to all real estate and other property and rights owned by each entity that is a party to the merger is vested in the surviving entity without reversion or impairment.

(c) The surviving entity may use the name and the assumed names of any entity that is a party to the merger, if the filings required under section 217(3) or (4) or any other applicable statute are made.

(d) The surviving entity has all of the liabilities of each entity that is a party to the merger. This subdivision does not affect the liability, if any, of a person that was an obligated person with respect to an entity that is a party to the merger for acts or omissions that occurred before the merger.

(e) A person may continue any proceeding that is pending against any entity that was a party to the merger as if the merger did not occur, or the surviving entity may be substituted in the proceeding for the entity whose existence ceased.

(f) The articles of incorporation of a surviving domestic corporation are amended to the extent provided in the plan of merger.

(g) The ownership interests, shares, or memberships of each entity that is a party to the merger that are to be converted into ownership interests or obligations of or membership or other interests in the surviving entity or into cash or other property are converted.

(6) If the surviving entity in a merger under this section is a foreign business organization, it is subject to the laws of this state pertaining to the transaction of business in this state if it transacts business in this state. The surviving entity is liable, and is subject to service of process in a proceeding in this state, for the enforcement of an obligation of a domestic corporation that is a party to the merger.

(7) Notwithstanding this section or any other provisions of this act, a corporation shall make distributions to its shareholders or members or to any other person in connection with a merger with a business organization under this section only in conformity with section 301 and with any limitations on distributions in its articles of incorporation.

(8) Section 735, and not this section, applies to a merger if all of the business organizations merging with 1 or more domestic corporations are foreign corporations, domestic business corporations, or foreign business corporations.

(9) As used in this section:

(a) "Business organization" means a domestic or foreign limited liability company, limited partnership, general partnership, or any other type of domestic or foreign business enterprise, incorporated or unincorporated, except a domestic business corporation, foreign corporation, or foreign business corporation.

(b) "Entity" means a business organization, domestic corporation, foreign corporation, or foreign business corporation.

(c) "Obligated person" means a general partner of a limited partnership, a partner of a general partnership, or a participant in or an owner of an interest in any other type of business enterprise that, under applicable law, is generally liable for the obligations of the business enterprise.

450.2741 Abandonment of merger; procedure; certificate of abandonment.
Sec. 741.

At any time before the effective date of the certificate of merger, subject to any contractual rights, a corporation may abandon a merger without further shareholder or member action, under a procedure set forth in the plan of merger or, if the plan of merger does not include an abandonment procedure, in the manner determined by the board. If a certificate of merger was filed by a corporation that abandons a merger, it shall file a certificate of abandonment within 10 days after the abandonment, but not later than the proposed effective date.

450.2745 Conversion of domestic corporation into business organization; requirements; effect; surviving business organization; liability for certain obligation; distributions; "business organization" and "entity" defined.
Sec. 745.

(1) A domestic corporation may convert into a business organization if all of the following requirements are satisfied:
(a) The conversion is permitted under the law that will govern the internal affairs of the business organization after conversion and the surviving business organization complies with that law in converting.
(b) Unless subdivision (d) applies, the board of the domestic corporation that is proposing to convert adopts a plan of conversion that includes all of the following:
(i) The name of the domestic corporation, the name of the business organization into which the domestic corporation is converting, the type of business organization into which the domestic corporation is converting, identification of the statute that will govern the internal affairs of the surviving business organization, the street address of the surviving business organization, the street address of the domestic corporation if it is different from the street address of the surviving business organization, and the principal place of business of the surviving business organization.
(ii) For a domestic corporation that is organized on a stock basis, the designation and number of outstanding shares of each class, specifying the classes that are entitled to vote, each class that is entitled to vote as a class, and, if the number of shares is subject to change before the effective date of the conversion, the manner in which the change may occur.

(iii) For a domestic corporation that is organized on a membership basis, a description of the members, including the number, classification, and voting rights of members.

(iv) For a domestic corporation that is organized on a directorship basis, a description of the organization of the board, including the number, classification, and voting rights of directors.

(v) The terms and conditions of the proposed conversion, including the manner and basis of converting the shares or memberships into ownership interests, or obligations of the surviving business organization, into cash, into other consideration that may include ownership interests or obligations of an entity that is not a party to the conversion, or into a combination of cash and other consideration.

(vi) The terms and conditions of the organizational documents that are to govern the surviving business organization.

(vii) Any other provisions with respect to the proposed conversion that the board considers necessary or desirable.

(c) If the board adopts the plan of conversion under subdivision (b), the plan of conversion is submitted for approval in the manner required for a merger under section 703a(2).

(d) If the domestic corporation has not commenced business, has not issued any shares or memberships, and has not elected a board, subdivisions (b) and (c) do not apply and the incorporators may approve the conversion of the corporation into a business organization by unanimous consent. To effect the conversion, a majority of the incorporators must execute and file a certificate of conversion under subdivision (e).

(e) After the plan of conversion is approved under subdivisions (b) and (c) or the conversion is approved under subdivision (d), the domestic corporation files any formation documents required to be filed under the laws that govern the internal affairs of the surviving business organization, in the manner required by those laws, and files a certificate of conversion with the administrator. The certificate of conversion shall include all of the following:

(i) Unless subdivision (d) applies, all of the information described in subdivision (b)(i), (ii), (iii), and (iv) and the manner and basis for converting the shares or memberships, if any, of the domestic corporation included in the plan of conversion.

(ii) Unless subdivision (d) applies, a statement that the board has adopted the plan of conversion under subdivision (c), or if subdivision (d) applies to the conversion, a statement that the domestic corporation has not commenced business, has not issued any shares or memberships, and has not elected a board and that the conversion was approved by the unanimous consent of the incorporators.

      (iii) A statement that the surviving business organization will furnish a copy of the plan of conversion, on request and without cost, to any shareholder or member of the domestic corporation.

      (iv) If approval of the shareholders or members of the domestic corporation is required, a statement that the plan was approved by the shareholders or members under subdivision (c).

      (v) A statement specifying each assumed name of the domestic corporation to be used by the surviving business organization and authorized under section 217(5).

(2) Section 131 applies in determining when a certificate of conversion under this section becomes effective.

(3) When a conversion under this section takes effect, all of the following apply:

  (a) The domestic corporation converts into the surviving business organization, and the articles of incorporation of the domestic corporation are canceled. Except as otherwise provided in this section, the surviving business organization is organized under and subject to the organizational laws of the jurisdiction of the surviving business organization as stated in the certificate of conversion.

  (b) The surviving business organization has all of the liabilities of the domestic corporation. The conversion of the domestic corporation into a business organization under this section does not affect any obligations or liabilities of the domestic corporation before conversion or the personal liability of any person that is incurred before the conversion, and the conversion shall not be considered to affect the choice of law applicable to the domestic corporation with respect to matters that arise before the conversion.

  (c) The title to all real estate and other property and rights owned by the domestic corporation is vested in the surviving business organization without reversion or impairment. The rights, privileges, powers, and interests in property of the domestic corporation, and the debts, liabilities, and duties of the domestic corporation, shall not be considered, as a consequence of the conversion, as transferred to the surviving business corporation to which the domestic corporation has converted for any purposes of the laws of this state.

  (d) The surviving business organization may use the name and assumed names of the domestic corporation if the filings required under section 217(5) or any other applicable statute are made and the laws regarding use and form of names are followed.

  (e) A person may continue any proceeding that is pending against the domestic corporation as if the conversion had not occurred, or the surviving business organization may be substituted in the proceeding for the domestic corporation.

  (f) The surviving business organization is considered to be the same entity that existed before the conversion and is considered to be organized on the date that the domestic corporation was originally incorporated.

(g) The shares or memberships of the domestic corporation that are to be converted into ownership interests or obligations of the surviving business organization or into cash or other property are converted.

(h) Unless otherwise provided in the plan of conversion, the domestic corporation is not required to wind up its affairs or pay its liabilities and distribute its assets on account of the conversion, and the conversion does not constitute a dissolution of the domestic corporation.

(4) If the surviving business organization of a conversion under this section is a foreign business organization, it is subject to the laws of this state pertaining to the transaction of business and the conduct of affairs in this state if it transacts business or conducts affairs in this state. The surviving business organization is liable, and is subject to service of process in a proceeding in this state, for the enforcement of an obligation of the domestic corporation.

(5) Notwithstanding this section and other provisions of this act, a corporation shall make distributions to shareholders or members of any corporation or to any other person in connection with a conversion under this section only in conformity with section 301 and with limitations on distributions in its articles of incorporation.

(6) As used in this section and section 746, "business organization" and "entity" mean those terms as defined in section 736a(9).

450.2746 Conversion of business organization into domestic corporation; requirements; effectiveness of certificate of conversion; surviving domestic corporation.
Sec. 746.

(1) A business organization may convert into a domestic corporation if all of the following requirements are satisfied:

(a) The conversion is permitted under the law that governs the internal affairs of the business organization and the business organization complies with that law in converting.

(b) The business organization that is proposing to convert into a domestic corporation adopts a plan of conversion that includes all of the following:

(i) The name of the business organization, the type of business organization that is converting, identification of the statute that governs the internal affairs of the business organization, the name of the surviving domestic corporation into which the business organization is converting, the street address of the surviving domestic corporation, and the principal place of business of the surviving domestic corporation.

(ii) A description of all of the ownership interests in the business organization, specifying the interests that are entitled to vote, any right those interests have to vote collectively or as a class, and, if the ownership interests are subject to change before the effective date of the conversion, the manner in which the change may occur.

      (iii) The terms and conditions of the proposed conversion, including the manner and basis of converting the ownership interests of the business organization into shares, memberships, or obligations of the surviving domestic corporation, into cash, into other consideration that may include ownership interests or obligations of an entity that is not a party to the conversion, or into a combination of cash and other consideration.

      (iv) The terms and conditions of the articles and bylaws that are to govern the surviving domestic corporation.

      (v) Any other provisions with respect to the proposed conversion that the business organization considers necessary or desirable.

(c) If the plan of conversion is adopted by the business organization under subdivision (b), the plan of conversion is submitted for approval in the manner required under the law governing the internal affairs of that business organization.

(d) After the plan of conversion is approved under subdivisions (b) and (c), the business organization files a certificate of conversion with the administrator. The certificate of conversion shall include all of the following:

      (i) All of the information described in subdivision (b)(i) and (ii) and the manner and basis of converting the ownership interests of the business organization included in the plan of conversion.

      (ii) A statement that the business organization has adopted the plan of conversion under subdivision (c).

      (iii) A statement that the surviving corporation will furnish a copy of the plan of conversion, on request and without cost, to any owner of the business organization.

      (iv) A statement specifying each assumed name of the business organization to be used by the surviving domestic corporation and authorized under section 217(6).

      (v) Articles of incorporation of the surviving domestic corporation that meet all of the requirements of this act applicable to articles of incorporation.

(2) Section 131 applies in determining when a certificate of conversion under this section becomes effective.

(3) When a business organization converts into a surviving domestic corporation under this section, all of the following apply:

(a) The business organization converts to the surviving domestic corporation. Except as otherwise provided in this section, the surviving domestic corporation is organized under and subject to this act.

(b) The surviving domestic corporation has all of the liabilities of the business organization. The conversion of the business organization into a domestic corporation under this section does not affect any obligations or liabilities of the business organization that are incurred before the conversion or the personal liability of any person that is incurred before the conversion and the conversion shall not be considered to affect the choice of law applicable to the business organization with respect to matters that arise before conversion.

(c) The title to all real estate and other property and rights owned by the business organization is vested in the surviving domestic corporation without reversion or impairment. The rights, privileges, powers, and interests in property of the business organization, and the debts, liabilities, and duties of the business organization, shall not be considered, as a consequence of the conversion, as transferred to the surviving domestic corporation to which the business organization has converted for any purpose under the laws of this state.

(d) The surviving domestic corporation may use the name and the assumed names of the business organization if the filings required under section 217(6) or any other applicable statute are made and the laws regarding the use and form of names are followed.

(e) A person may continue any proceeding that is pending against the business organization as if the conversion had not occurred, or the surviving domestic corporation may be substituted in the proceeding for the business organization.

(f) The surviving domestic corporation is considered to be the same entity that existed before the conversion and is considered to be organized on the date that the business organization was originally organized.

(g) The ownership interests of the business organization that were converted into shares, memberships, or obligations of the surviving domestic corporation or into cash or other property are converted.

(h) Unless otherwise provided in the plan of conversion, the business organization is not required to wind up its affairs or pay its liabilities and distribute its assets on account of the conversion, and the conversion does not constitute a dissolution of the business organization.

450.2751 Actions by corporation; terms and conditions; consideration; "consideration" defined.
Sec. 751.

(1) A corporation may take any of the following actions on the terms and conditions and for a consideration authorized by its board of directors:

(a) Sell, lease, exchange, or otherwise dispose of all, or substantially all, of its property and assets in the usual and regular course of its business.

(b) Sell, lease, exchange, or otherwise dispose of all, or substantially all, of its property and assets following approval of a dissolution under section 804.

(c) Transfer any or all of its property and assets to another corporation of which it owns all of the shares, or to another entity that it controls or wholly owns, whether or not in the usual and regular course of business.

(d) Mortgage or pledge any or all of its property and assets, whether or not in the usual and regular course of business.

(2) Unless otherwise provided in the articles of incorporation, approval by the shareholders or members of a transaction described in subsection (1) is not required.

(3) As used in subsection (1), "consideration" may consist in whole or in part of cash or other property, including shares, bonds, or other securities of any other domestic corporation, domestic business corporation, foreign corporation, or foreign business corporation.

450.2753 Disposition of property and assets of corporation; disposal of all or substantially all of property; presumption that corporation retains significant continuing business activity; "consideration" defined; recommendation of proposed transaction; exceptions; submission to shareholders or members; approval; notice of meeting; statement; authorization; fixing term or condition and consideration; voting; abandonment; distribution.
Sec. 753.

(1) Except as provided in section 751, a corporation may sell, lease, exchange, or otherwise dispose of all, or substantially all, of its property and assets, with or without the goodwill, in a transaction that is not in the usual and regular course of its business, on any terms and conditions and for any consideration that is authorized under this section. A corporation has not disposed of all or substantially all of its property and assets under this subsection if it retains a significant continuing business activity. For purposes of this subsection, it is conclusively presumed that a corporation has retained a significant continuing business activity if the corporation and its subsidiaries reported on a consolidated basis continue to conduct an activity that represented at least 25% of total revenues or 25% of total assets at the end of the most recently completed fiscal year or at least 25% of total program expenditures for that fiscal year. As used in this subsection, "consideration" may consist in whole or in part of cash or other property, including shares, bonds, or other securities of any other domestic corporation, domestic business corporation, foreign corporation, or foreign business corporation.

(2) The board of a stock or membership corporation must recommend a proposed transaction described in subsection (1) to the shareholders or members, unless any of the following apply:
   (a) The board determines that because of a conflict of interest, events that occur after the board adopts the plan, contractual obligations, or other special circumstances it should make no recommendation.
   (b) The power to initiate the transaction is reserved to the shareholders or members without action of the board in the articles of incorporation or in an agreement under section 488.
   (c) Section 529 applies.

(3) If 1 or more of the exceptions in subsection (2) apply, the board must communicate the basis for not making a recommendation to the shareholders or members.

(4) The board may condition its submission to shareholders or members under subsection (2) on any basis.

(5) If a corporation is organized on a stock or membership basis, the corporation must submit a proposed transaction described in subsection (1) for approval at a meeting of shareholders or members. The corporation shall give notice of the meeting to each shareholder or member of record, whether or not that person is entitled to vote at the meeting, within the time and in the manner provided under this act for the giving of notice of meetings of shareholders or members. The notice shall include or be accompanied by a statement that summarizes the principal terms of the proposed transaction or a copy of any documents that contain the principal terms.

(6) At a meeting described in subsection (5), the shareholders or members may authorize the sale, lease, exchange, or other disposition and may fix, or may authorize the board to fix, any term or condition and the consideration to be received by the corporation for that transaction. Subject to subsections (8) and (9), the transaction is approved if a majority of the votes held by shareholders or members of the corporation entitled to vote are cast in favor of the sale, lease, exchange, or other disposition.

(7) Notwithstanding subsection (6), unless a greater vote is required in the articles of incorporation or in a bylaw adopted by the shareholders or members, if there are more than 20 shareholders or members that are entitled to vote at the meeting, the sale, lease, exchange, or other disposition is approved if a majority of the votes held by shareholders or members that are present in person or by proxy at the meeting are cast in favor of the sale, lease, exchange, or other disposition.

(8) Notwithstanding authorization by the shareholders or members under subsection (5) or (6), unless the power to initiate the transaction is reserved to the shareholders or members without action of the board in the articles of incorporation or in an agreement under section 488, the board may abandon a sale, lease, exchange, or other disposition under subsection (1), subject to the rights of third parties under any contracts that relate to the sale, lease, exchange, or other disposition, without further action or approval by shareholders or members.

(9) If a corporation is organized on a directorship basis, a sale, lease, exchange, or other disposition of all, or substantially all, of the property and assets, with or without goodwill, of a corporation, in a transaction that is not in the usual and regular course of its business, is authorized if it receives the affirmative vote of a majority of the directors who are then in office. A corporation shall give notice of the meeting to authorize a sale, lease, exchange, or other disposition under this subsection to each director who is then in office at least 20 days before the meeting, and the notice shall include a statement that summarizes the principal terms of the proposed transaction or a copy of any documents that contain the principal terms.

(10) A sale, lease, exchange, or other disposition of all, or substantially all, of the property and assets of a corporation or other entity of which a second corporation owns a majority of the shares or beneficial interests, including a

change in shares of the corporation or beneficial interest in another entity held by the second corporation because of a merger, is a disposition by the second corporation of its pro rata share of the property and assets of the corporation or other entity on a consolidated basis for purposes of this section.

(11) A transaction that is a distribution permitted under section 301 is governed by section 545, and this section and section 751 do not apply to that transaction.

450.2754 Merger or acquisition under MCL 2703a(2); right of shareholders or members to receive notice and vote.
Sec. 754.

Shareholders or members of a corporation that proposes to issue, directly or through a subsidiary, its shares, memberships, obligations, or securities in the course of a merger, acquisition of some or all of the outstanding shares of another corporation or interests in or memberships of another entity, or acquisition of some or all of the assets other than cash of a corporation or other entity have the rights to receive notice and to vote on the proposed merger or acquisition provided under section 703a(2) if both of the following apply:

   (a) The securities or other interests to be issued or delivered in the acquisition are or may be converted into shares or memberships of the acquiring corporation.

   (b) The number of the acquiring corporation's voting shares or member votes to be issued or delivered, plus those initially issuable on the conversion or exchange of any other securities to be issued or delivered, will exceed 100% of the number of its voting shares or member votes outstanding immediately before the acquisition plus the number of its common shares or memberships, if any, initially issuable on the conversion or exchange of any other securities that are then outstanding.

Chapter 8 – Dissolution and Reorganization

450.2801 Dissolution of corporation; methods; summary dissolution of corporation whose assets disposed of under court order in receivership or bankruptcy proceedings; filing copy of order with administrator.
Sec. 801.

(1) A corporation may be dissolved in any of the following ways:

   (a) Automatically by expiration of a period of duration to which the corporation is limited in its articles of incorporation.

   (b) By action of the incorporators or directors under section 803.

   (c) By action of the shareholders, members, or the board under section 804.

(d) Pursuant to an agreement under section 488. A dissolution under this subdivision becomes effective by filing a certificate under section 805.

(e) By a judgment of the circuit court in an action that is brought under this act or otherwise.

(f) Automatically, under section 922, for failure to file an annual report or pay an annual filing fee.

(2) A corporation whose assets have been wholly disposed of under court order in receivership or bankruptcy proceedings may be summarily dissolved by order of the court that has jurisdiction of the proceedings. The clerk of the court shall file a copy of the order with the administrator.

450.2803 Dissolution of corporation by action of incorporators or directors; conditions; certificate of dissolution.
Sec. 803.

(1) A corporation may be dissolved by action of its incorporators or directors, if the corporation complies with all of the following conditions:
   (a) Has not commenced affairs.
   (b) Has not issued any shares and has no members entitled to vote on dissolution.
   (c) Has no debts or other liabilities.
   (d) Has received no payments on subscriptions for its shares or memberships, contributions or other funds from members or third parties, or, if it has received payments, has returned them to those entitled thereto, less any part thereof disbursed for expenses.

(2) The dissolution of the corporation shall be effected by a majority of the incorporators or directors, executing and filing a certificate of dissolution stating:
   (a) The name of the corporation.
   (b) That the corporation has not commenced affairs, has issued no shares, and has no members entitled to vote on dissolution, and has no debts or other liabilities.
   (c) That the corporation has received no payments on subscriptions to its shares or memberships, contributions or other funds from members or third parties, or, if it has received payments, has returned them to those entitled thereto, less any part thereof disbursed for expenses.
   (d) That a majority of the incorporators or directors have elected that the corporation be dissolved.

450.2804 Dissolution of corporation by action of shareholders or members; recommendation; exceptions; approval or authorization; notice; voting; certificate.
Sec. 804.

(1) A corporation may be dissolved by action of its board and its shareholders or members, if any, as provided in this section.

(2) The board of a corporation that is organized on a stock or membership basis may propose dissolution for action by the shareholders or members.

(3) The board of a corporation that is organized on a stock or membership basis must recommend a dissolution under this section to the shareholders or members unless any of the following apply:

    (a) The board determines that because of a conflict of interest or other special circumstances it should make no recommendation.

    (b) The power to dissolve the corporation is reserved to the shareholders or members without action of the board in the articles of incorporation or in an agreement under section 488.

    (c) Section 529 applies.

(4) If 1 or more of the exceptions described in subsection (3) apply, the board must communicate to the shareholders or members the basis for not making a recommendation.

(5) The board may condition its submission of a proposal for dissolution to shareholders or members under subsection (3) on any basis.

(6) If a corporation is organized on a stock or membership basis, the board shall submit a proposed dissolution for approval at a meeting of shareholders or members. The corporation shall give notice to each shareholder or member of record, whether or not that person is entitled to vote at the meeting, within the time and in the manner provided under this act for the giving of notice of meetings of shareholders or members. The notice shall state that a purpose of the meeting is to vote on dissolution of the corporation.

(7) At a meeting described in subsection (6), the shareholders or members shall vote on the proposed dissolution. Except as provided in this subsection, a dissolution is approved if a majority of the votes held by shareholders or members of the corporation that are entitled to vote on the proposed dissolution are cast in favor of dissolution. Unless a greater vote is required in the articles of incorporation or in a bylaw adopted by the shareholders or members, if there are more than 20 members or shareholders that are entitled to vote at the meeting, dissolution is approved if a majority of the votes held by shareholders or members that are entitled to vote on the proposed dissolution present in person or by proxy at the meeting are cast in favor of dissolution.

(8) If a corporation is organized on a directorship basis, a dissolution is approved if it receives the affirmative vote of a majority of directors who are then in office. The corporation shall give notice of the meeting to authorize the dissolution to each director who is then in office at least 10 days before the meeting, and the notice shall state that a purpose of the meeting is to vote on dissolution of the corporation.

(9) If the dissolution is approved, a certificate of dissolution shall be executed and submitted on behalf of the corporation, setting forth:

    (a) The name of the corporation.

    (b) The date and place of the meeting of shareholders, members, or directors at which the dissolution was approved.

(c) A statement that dissolution was proposed and approved by the requisite vote of directors and the shareholders or members under subsection (7), or the directors under subsection (8).

450.2805 Dissolution under agreement under MCL 450.2488; effectiveness.
Sec. 805.

Dissolution under an agreement under section 488 becomes effective by executing and filing a certificate of dissolution on behalf of the corporation that states the name of the corporation and that the corporation is dissolved under an agreement under section 488.

450.2811 Revocation of dissolution proceedings; filing and execution of certificate; additional manner of revocation.
Sec. 811.

(1) A corporation may revoke dissolution proceedings commenced under section 488 or 804 before complete distribution of assets, if a proceeding under section 851 is not pending, by filing a certificate of revocation that is executed, in person or by proxy, by all the shareholders, members, or directors that are entitled to vote on dissolution, and states that the revocation is effective under this section and that all the shareholders, members, or directors of the corporation that are entitled to vote on dissolution have executed the certificate in person or by proxy.

(2) In addition to revoking a dissolution under subsection (1), a corporation may also revoke dissolution proceedings commenced under section 804 before complete distribution of assets, if a proceeding under section 851 is not pending, in the following manner:

(a) Unless the power to dissolve the corporation is reserved to the shareholders or members without action of the board in the articles of incorporation or in an agreement under section 488, the board of directors shall adopt a resolution revoking dissolution. The corporation shall submit the proposed revocation for approval at a meeting of shareholders or members. The corporation shall give the shareholders or members the same notice of the meeting and the revocation must be approved by the same vote that is required under section 804 for the approval of dissolution.

(b) If the power to dissolve the corporation is reserved to the shareholders or members without action of the board in the articles of incorporation or in an agreement under section 488, the shareholders or members may approve revocation of dissolution in the manner provided in the articles of incorporation or in the agreement under section 488 for approval of dissolution. The corporation shall give the shareholders or members the same notice of the meeting that is required under section 804 for the approval of dissolution and the revocation of dissolution must be approved by the same vote that is required under section 804 or in the applicable provisions of the articles of incorporation or in the agreement under section 488 for the approval of dissolution.

(c) If the corporation is organized on a directorship basis, a dissolution may be revoked by the affirmative vote of a majority of the directors who are then in office. The corporation shall give the directors the same notice of the meeting that is required in section 804 for dissolution.

(d) A certificate of revocation, that states that dissolution is revoked under this section, and includes the information required under section 804(8), shall be executed and filed on behalf of the corporation.

450.2815 Renewal of corporate existence.
Sec. 815.

A corporation whose term has expired may renew its corporate existence, if a proceeding under section 851 is not pending, in the following manner:

(a) The board adopts a resolution to renew the corporation's corporate existence.

(b) If the corporation is organized on a stock or membership basis, the corporation submits the proposed renewal for approval at a meeting of shareholders or members. The corporation shall give notice to each shareholder or member of record that is entitled to vote at the meeting within the time and in the manner provided under this act for the giving of notice of meetings of shareholders or members. The notice shall state that a purpose of the meeting is to vote on the renewal of corporate existence. At the meeting, shareholders or members that are entitled to vote on the renewal shall vote on the proposed renewal and the renewal is adopted if a majority of the votes held by shareholders or members of the corporation that are entitled to vote on the renewal are cast in favor of the renewal. Unless a greater vote is required in the articles of incorporation or in a bylaw adopted by the shareholders or members, a proposed renewal is also adopted if a majority of votes that are held by shareholders or members present in person or by proxy at the meeting are cast in favor of the renewal and due notice of the time, place, and object of the meeting is given by mail, at the last known address, to each shareholder or member that is entitled to vote on the renewal at least 20 days before the date of the meeting or by publication in a publication distributed to its shareholders or members at least 20 days before the date of the meeting.

(c) If the corporation is organized on a directorship basis, renewal is authorized if it receives the affirmative vote of a majority of directors who are then in office.

(d) If renewal of the corporate existence of a corporation is approved, a certificate of renewal shall be executed and filed on behalf of the corporation that includes all of the following:

(i) The name of the corporation.

(ii) The date and place of the meeting of shareholders or members at which the renewal of existence was approved, if any.

(iii) A statement that renewal was approved by the requisite vote of the directors and the shareholders or members under subdivision (b), or of the directors under subdivision (c).

(iv) The duration of the corporation, if other than perpetual.

450.2817 Effect of filing certificate of revocation of dissolution or renewal of corporate existence; accrued penalty or liability; adoption of corporate name; rights.
Sec. 817.

(1) When a certificate of revocation of dissolution is filed under section 811 or a certificate of renewal of existence is filed under section 815, the revocation of the dissolution proceedings or the renewal of the corporate existence becomes effective, and the corporation may again conduct affairs.

(2) Revocation of dissolution under section 811 or renewal of corporate existence under section 815 does not relieve a corporation of any penalty or liability accrued against it under any law of this state.

(3) The administrator may require a corporation that files a certificate of revocation of dissolution under section 811 or a certificate of renewal of corporate existence under section 815 to adopt a corporate name that conforms to the requirements of section 212.

(4) The rights of a corporation that complies with this section are the same as though a dissolution or expiration of term has not occurred, and all contracts entered into and other rights acquired during the interval are valid and enforceable.

450.2821 Action by attorney general for dissolution of corporation; grounds; other actions.
Sec. 821.

(1) The attorney general may bring an action in the circuit court for the county in which the principal place of business or registered office of a corporation is located or for Ingham county for dissolution of a corporation on the ground that the corporation has committed any of the following acts:

(a) Procured its organization through fraud.

(b) Repeatedly, willfully, and materially exceeded the authority conferred on it by law.

(c) Repeatedly, willfully, and materially conducted its affairs in an unlawful manner.

(2) The enumeration in this section of grounds for dissolution does not exclude any other statutory or common law action by the attorney general for dissolution of a corporation or revocation or forfeiture of its corporate franchises.

450.2823 Dissolution of corporation by judgment in action brought in court; proof; action for dissolution of charitable purpose corporation.
Sec. 823.

(1) A corporation that is organized on a stock or membership basis may be dissolved by a judgment entered in an action brought in the circuit court for the county in which the principal place of business or registered office of the corporation is located by 1 or more directors or by 1 or more shareholders or members that are entitled to vote in an election of directors of the corporation, if both of the following are proved:
  (a) The directors of the corporation, or its shareholders or members if a provision in the articles of incorporation authorized under section 488(1) is in effect, are unable to agree by the requisite vote on material matters respecting management of the corporation's affairs, or the shareholders or members of the corporation are so divided in voting power that they have failed to elect a successor for any director whose term has expired or would have expired on the election and qualification of his or her successor.
  (b) As a result of a condition stated in subdivision (a), the corporation is unable to carry out its corporate purposes or function effectively in the best interests of its creditors and shareholders or members, if any, or the persons that the corporation is organized to benefit.
(2) A corporation that is organized on a directorship basis may be dissolved by a judgment entered in an action brought in the circuit court for the county in which the principal place of business or registered office of the corporation is located by 1 or more directors or by 1 or more other persons that are entitled to vote in an election of 1 or more of the directors of the corporation, if both of the following are proved:
  (a) The directors of the corporation are unable to agree by the requisite vote on material matters respecting management of the corporation's affairs, or the directors or other persons that are entitled to vote in the election of 1 or more of the directors of the corporation are so divided in voting power that they have failed to elect a successor for any director whose term has expired or would have expired on the election and qualification of his or her successor.
  (b) As a result of a condition stated in subdivision (a), the corporation is unable to carry out its corporate purposes or function effectively in the best interests of its creditors and shareholders or members, if any, or the persons that the corporation is organized to benefit.
(3) A person or persons that files an action for dissolution of a charitable purpose corporation under this section shall give the attorney general written notice of the commencement of the action by mail within 30 days after filing.

450.2831 Dissolution of corporation; conditions.
Sec. 831.

A corporation is dissolved when any of the following occurs:
  (a) The period of duration stated in the corporation's articles of incorporation expires.
  (b) A certificate of dissolution is filed pursuant to sections 803 to 805.
  (c) A judgment of forfeiture of corporate franchises or of dissolution is entered by a court of competent jurisdiction and a copy of a judicial order of dissolution shall be forwarded promptly to the administrator by the receiver or other person designated by the court.
  (d) Failure to file an annual report or pay an annual filing fee, as provided in section 922.

450.2833 Dissolved corporation; continuation of corporate existence; conduct of affairs.
Sec. 833.

Except as a court may otherwise direct, a dissolved corporation shall continue its corporate existence but shall not conduct affairs except for the purpose of winding up its affairs by:
  (a) Collecting its assets.
  (b) Selling or otherwise transferring, with or without security, assets which are not to be distributed in kind pursuant to section 855.
  (c) Paying its debts and other liabilities.
  (d) Doing all other acts incident to liquidation of its affairs.

450.2834 Dissolved corporation and officers, directors, shareholders, and members; manner of functioning.
Sec. 834.

Subject to section 833 and except as otherwise provided by court order, a dissolved corporation, its officers, directors, shareholders, and members shall continue to function in the same manner as if dissolution had not occurred. Without limiting the generality of this section:
  (a) The directors of the corporation are not deemed to be trustees of its assets solely because of the fact of dissolution and shall thereby be held to no greater standard of conduct than that prescribed by section 541.
  (b) Title to the corporation's assets remains in the corporation until transferred by it in the corporate name.
  (c) The dissolution does not change quorum or voting requirements for the board, shareholders, or members and does not alter provisions regarding election, appointment, resignation or removal of, or filling vacancies among, directors or officers, or provisions regarding amendment or repeal of bylaws or adoption of new bylaws.
  (d) Shares may be transferred if otherwise authorized.

    (e) The corporation may sue and be sued in its corporate name and process may issue by and against the corporation in the same manner as if dissolution had not occurred.

    (f) An action brought against the corporation before its dissolution does not abate because of the dissolution.

450.2841a Written notice to claimants of dissolved corporation.
Sec. 841a.

(1) A dissolved corporation may notify its existing claimants in writing of the dissolution of the corporation at any time after the effective date of the dissolution. The written notice shall include all of the following:

    (a) A description of the information that must be included in a claim. The corporation may demand sufficient information to permit it to make a reasonable judgment whether the claim should be accepted or rejected.

    (b) A mailing address where a claim may be sent.

    (c) The deadline by which the dissolved corporation must receive the claim. The deadline must be at least 6 months after the effective date of the written notice.

    (d) A statement that a claim that is not received by the deadline is barred.

(2) Providing a notice under subsection (1) does not constitute recognition that a person to which the notice is directed has a valid claim against the corporation.

(3) A claim against a dissolved corporation is barred if either of the following applies:

    (a) If a claimant that was given written notice under subsection (1) does not deliver the claim to the dissolved corporation by the deadline.

    (b) If a claimant whose claim is rejected by a written notice of rejection by the dissolved corporation does not commence a proceeding to enforce the claim within 90 days after the effective date of the written notice of rejection.

(4) As used in this section and section 842a:

    (a) The "effective date" of a written notice is the earliest of the following:

        (i) The date it is received.

        (ii) Five days after its deposit in the United States mail, as evidenced by the postmark, if it is mailed postpaid and correctly addressed.

        (iii) The date shown on the return receipt, if the notice is sent by registered or certified mail, return receipt requested, and the receipt is signed by or on behalf of the addressee.

    (b) "Existing claim" means any claim or right against a corporation, liquidated or unliquidated. The term does not mean a contingent liability or a claim that is based on an event that occurs after the effective date of dissolution of the corporation.

450.2842a Publication of notice of dissolved corporation.
Sec. 842a.

(1) In addition to providing notice under section 841a, a dissolved corporation may also publish notice of dissolution at any time after the effective date of dissolution and request that persons with claims against the corporation present them in the manner described in the notice.

(2) A notice described in subsection (1) must meet both of the following:
  (a) Be published 1 time in a newspaper of general circulation in the county where the dissolved corporation's principal office, or if there is no principal office in this state, its registered office, is or was last located.
  (b) State that a claim against the corporation is barred unless a proceeding to enforce the claim is commenced within 1 year after the publication date of the newspaper notice.

(3) Subject to subsection (4), if a dissolved corporation publishes a newspaper notice under subsection (2), the claim of each of the following claimants is barred unless the claimant commences a proceeding to enforce the claim against the dissolved corporation within 1 year after the publication date of the newspaper notice:
  (a) A claimant that did not receive written notice under section 841a.
  (b) A claimant that sent a timely claim to the dissolved corporation but the corporation did not act on the claim.
  (c) A claimant whose claim is contingent or based on an event that occurs after the effective date of dissolution.

(4) Notwithstanding subsection (3), a claimant that has an existing claim that is known to the corporation at the time of publication under subsection (2) and that did not receive written notice under section 841a is not barred from commencing a proceeding until 6 months after the claimant has actual notice of the dissolution.

450.2851 Application for judgment that affairs of corporation and liquidation of assets continue under supervision of court; orders and judgments; permitting creditor to file claim or commence proceeding.
Sec. 851.

(1) After a corporation is dissolved in any manner, the corporation, a creditor, a shareholder, member, or a director may apply at any time to the circuit court in the county in which the principal place of business or registered office of the corporation is located for a judgment that the affairs of the corporation and the liquidation of its assets continue under supervision of the court. The court shall make any orders and judgments that are required, including, but not limited to, continuance of the liquidation of the corporation's assets by its officers and directors under supervision of the court, or the appointment of a receiver of the corporation that is vested with powers that the court designates to liquidate the affairs of the corporation.

(2) For good cause shown, and if a corporation has not made complete distribution of its assets, the court may permit a creditor that has a claim

against the corporation and has not delivered that claim to the corporation or commenced a proceeding to enforce the claim within the time limits under sections 841a and 842a, or who has not commenced an action on a rejected claim within the time limits under sections 841a and 842a, to file the claim or to commence a proceeding within the time that the court directs.

450.2855 Dissolution of corporation; applicable provisions.
Sec. 855.

(1) All of the following apply if a corporation is dissolved:
   (a) The corporation shall pay or make provision for its debts, obligations, and liabilities. Compliance with this subdivision requires that, to the extent that a reasonable estimate is possible, provision is made for those debts, obligations, and liabilities that are anticipated to arise after the effective date of dissolution. A corporation is not required to make provision for any debt, obligation, or liability that is or is reasonably anticipated to be barred under section 841a or 842a. The fact that corporate assets are insufficient to satisfy claims that arise after a dissolution does not create a presumption that the corporation has failed to comply with this subdivision. A corporation is considered to have made adequate provision for any debt, obligation, or liability of the corporation if payment is assumed or guaranteed in good faith by 1 or more financially responsible corporations, other persons, or the United States government or an agency of the United States government and the provision, including the financial responsibility of the corporations or other persons, was determined in good faith and with reasonable care by the board to be adequate.
   (b) If the corporation holds any assets subject to a condition that requires return, transfer, or conveyance, and the condition occurs by reason of the dissolution, the corporation shall return, transfer, or convey those assets in compliance with those conditions.
   (c) If the corporation received and holds any assets that are subject to limitations that permit their use only for charitable, religious, eleemosynary, benevolent, educational, or similar purposes, but that are not held subject to a condition that requires return, transfer, or conveyance by reason of the dissolution under subdivision (b), the corporative shall transfer or convey those assets in a manner that complies with any provisions in the articles of incorporation or bylaws that designate 1 or more recipients or establish a mechanism for determining 1 or more recipients that are domestic or foreign corporations, societies, or organizations, including governmental agencies, that are engaged in activities that further those purposes. If the articles of incorporation or bylaws do not contain a provision described in this subdivision, the corporation shall transfer or convey those assets to 1 or more domestic or foreign corporations, societies, or organizations, including governmental agencies, that are engaged in

activities that are substantially similar to or consistent with those of the dissolving corporation.

(d) The corporation shall distribute any other assets in a manner that complies with any provisions of the articles of incorporation or the bylaws that determine the distributive rights of shareholders or members, or any class or classes of shareholders or members, or provide for distribution to others. Except as otherwise provided in this section, the corporation may distribute assets that are subject to this subdivision in cash, in kind, or both in cash and in kind, to shareholders, members, or others according to their respective rights and interests.

(e) The corporation distributes any remaining assets to any persons specified in a plan of distribution adopted by the corporation.

(2) If any assets of a dissolved corporation are not subject to any provision for the distribution of assets described in subsection (1), those remaining escheat to the state.

450.2861 Plan of reorganization; action by directors, shareholders, or members not required to put plan into effect.
Sec. 861.

A corporation for which a plan of reorganization has been confirmed by the judgment of a court of competent jurisdiction pursuant to any applicable law of this state or the United States may put into effect and carry out the plan without action by its directors, shareholders, or members. Such action may be taken as directed in the judgment by the receiver or trustee of the corporation appointed in the reorganization proceedings, or by any other person designated by the court.

450.2862 Powers of corporation under reorganization; issuing shares of capital stock and bonds for consideration specified in plan of reorganization.
Sec. 862.

(1) The corporation, in the manner provided in section 861, but without limiting the generality or effect of that section, may amend or repeal its bylaws; constitute or reconstitute and classify or reclassify its board of directors, and name, constitute, or appoint directors and officers in place of or in addition to any director or officer then in office; amend its articles of incorporation, and make any change in its capital or capital stock, or any other amendment, change, alteration, or provision, authorized by this act; be dissolved, transfer any part of its assets, and merge or consolidate as permitted by this act, change the location of its registered office, and remove or appoint a resident agent; authorize and fix the terms, manner, and conditions of the issuance of bonds, debentures, or other obligations, whether or not convertible into shares of its capital stock of any class, or

bearing warrants or other evidences of optional rights to purchase or subscribe for shares of its capital stock of any class, and lease its property and franchises.

(2) Irrespective of any other provision of this act, the corporation may issue its shares of capital stock and its bonds for the consideration specified in the plan of reorganization after confirmation of the plan.

450.2863 Document filed or recorded to accomplish corporate purpose pursuant to plan of reorganization; making, execution, and acknowledgment; contents; filing.
Sec. 863.

A certificate or other document required or permitted by law to be filed or recorded to accomplish any corporate purpose, sought to be accomplished pursuant to the plan of reorganization, shall be made, executed, and acknowledged, as may be directed by such judgment by the persons designated in section 861. The certificate or document shall certify that provision for the making of the certificate or document is contained in the plan of reorganization or in a judgment of a court having jurisdiction of the proceeding under such applicable statute of this state or of the United States for the reorganization of the corporation, and that the plan has been confirmed, as provided by such applicable statute, with the title and venue of the proceeding and the date of the judgment confirming the plan. The certificate or other document shall be filed as provided in section 131, and upon such filing becomes effective in accordance with the terms thereof and the provisions of sections 861 to 864.

450.2864 Reversal or vacation of reorganization plan; filing of other or further certificates or documents; effect; fees.
Sec. 864.

(1) If after the filing of a certificate or other document the order of confirmation of the plan of reorganization is reversed or vacated or the plan is modified, other or further certificates or documents shall be filed as required to conform to the plan of reorganization as finally confirmed or to the judgment of the court.
(2) Except as otherwise provided in sections 861 to 864, a certificate or other document filed pursuant to this section or section 863 is not deemed to confer on a corporation any power, privilege, or franchise, except those permitted to be conferred on a corporation formed or existing under this act.
(3) On the filing of a certificate or other document pursuant to this section or any other section of this act, the same fees shall be paid to the administrator as are payable by a corporation not in reorganization upon filing like certificates or documents.

Chapter 9 – Renewal and Reporting

450.2901 Report of domestic corporation; contents; electronic transmission; distribution to shareholder, member, or director.
Sec. 901.

(1) A domestic corporation at least once in each calendar year shall prepare or have prepared a report of the corporation for the preceding fiscal year and distribute that report to each shareholder or member or present the report at the annual meeting of shareholders or members or, if the corporation is organized on a directorship basis, at the annual meeting of the board. The report shall include all of the following for the corporation's preceding fiscal year:
   (a) Its income statement.
   (b) Its year-end balance sheet, including trust funds and funds restricted by donors or the board.
   (c) Its statement of source and application of funds, if the corporation prepares that statement.
   (d) Any other information required under this act.
(2) A corporation may distribute the financial report required under subsection (1) electronically, either by electronic transmission of the report or by making the report available for electronic transmission. If the report is distributed electronically under this subsection, the corporation shall provide the report in written form to a shareholder, member, or director on request.

450.2911 Annual report to administrator; filing; contents.
Sec. 911.

(1) Each domestic corporation and each foreign corporation authorized to conduct affairs in this state shall file a report with the administrator not later than October 1 of each year. The report shall be on a form approved by the administrator, signed by an authorized officer or agent of the corporation, and contain all of the following information:
   (a) The name of the corporation.
   (b) The name of its resident agent and address of its registered office in this state.
   (c) The names and business or residence addresses of its president, secretary, treasurer, and directors.
   (d) The purposes of the corporation.
   (e) The general nature and kind of business in which the corporation is engaged.
(2) A corporation is not required to file a report required under this section in the year of incorporation or authorization if the corporation was formed or authorized to do business on or after January 1 and before October 1 of that year.

(3) If there are no changes in the information provided in the last filed report required under subsection (1), the corporation may file a report that certifies to the administrator that no changes in the required information have occurred since the last filed report. A report filed under this subsection shall be on a form approved by the administrator and filed not later than the date required in subsection (1).

450.2913 Destruction or disposal of certain records.
Sec. 913.

A county clerk may destroy the copies of any corporate documents of a domestic or foreign corporation that were forwarded to his or her office under 1931 PA 327, MCL 450.98 to 450.192, any repealed provisions of 1931 PA 327, or its predecessor act. The clerk may destroy these records or dispose of them under section 5 of 1913 PA 271, MCL 399.5.

450.2922 Failure of domestic or foreign corporation to file annual report or pay filing fee or penalty; automatic dissolution or revocation of certificate of authority; dissolution of charitable purpose corporation; notice; right to certificate of good standing; electronic transmission of notification.
Sec. 922.

(1) If a domestic corporation neglects or refuses to file its annual report under section 911 or pay any annual filing fee or a penalty added to the fee required by law, and the neglect or refusal continues for a period of 2 years from the date on which the annual report or filing fee was due, the corporation is automatically dissolved 60 days after the expiration of the 2-year period. The administrator shall notify the corporation of the impending dissolution at least 90 days before the 2-year period expires. Until a corporation is dissolved under this subsection, it is entitled to issuance by the administrator, on request, of a certificate of good standing that states that the corporation was validly incorporated as a domestic corporation and that it is validly in existence under the laws of this state.
(2) A charitable purpose corporation that is dissolved under subsection (1) shall within 90 days after the date of the dissolution comply with the dissolution of charitable purpose corporation act, 1965 PA 169, MCL 450.251 to 450.253, or renew its corporate existence under section 925. This subsection does not prevent a corporation that is dissolved under subsection (1) from renewing its corporate existence under section 925 at any time.
(3) If a foreign corporation neglects or refuses for 1 year to file its annual report under section 911 or pay the annual filing fee required by law, its certificate of authority is subject to revocation under section 1042. Until revocation of its certificate of authority, or its withdrawal from this state or termination of its existence, the foreign corporation is entitled to issuance by the administrator, on request, of a certificate of good standing that states that it

was validly authorized to conduct affairs in this state and that it holds a valid certificate of authority to conduct affairs in this state.

(4) The administrator may electronically transmit a notification of pending dissolution described in subsection (1) to the resident agent of the corporation in the manner authorized by the corporation.

450.2923 Extension of time for filing report; reporting failure or neglect under MCL 450.2922, 450.2931, or 450.2932; action by attorney general; notice; electronic transmission.
Sec. 923.

(1) If good cause is shown, the administrator may extend the time for filing a report under section 911 for not more than 1 year after the due date of the filing.

(2) The administrator may report promptly to the attorney general any failure or neglect under sections 922, 931, or 932, and the attorney general may bring an action to impose the prescribed penalties. If a domestic or foreign corporation neglects or refuses to file its report under section 911 within the time required under this act, the administrator shall notify the corporation of that fact by mail sent to its registered office within 90 days after the due date of the filing.

(3) The administrator may electronically transmit a notification described in subsection (2) to the resident agent of the corporation in the manner authorized by the corporation.

450.2924 Annual reports due or deficient prior to date of act; penalties.
Sec. 924.

Annual reports due or deficient prior to the date of this act shall be subject to the penalties in effect at the statutory filing date.

450.2925 Renewal of corporate existence or certificate of authority following dissolution or revocation.
Sec. 925.

(1) A domestic corporation that is dissolved under section 922(1), or a foreign corporation whose certificate of authority is revoked under section 922(2) or section 1042, may renew its corporate existence or its certificate of authority by filing the annual reports under section 911 for the last 5 years or any lesser number of years in which the reports were not filed and paying the annual filing fees for all the years for which they were not paid, together with a penalty of $5.00 for each delinquent report. When the reports are filed and the fees and penalties are paid, the corporate existence or the certificate of authority is renewed. The administrator may require that the

corporation adopt or use in this state a corporate name that conforms to the requirements of section 212.

(2) The rights of a corporation that complies with this section are the same as if a dissolution or revocation has not taken place, and all contracts entered into and other rights acquired during the interval are valid and enforceable.

450.2931 Wilful false statement in report; additional penalty.
Sec. 931.

If a domestic or foreign corporation which is required to file a report as provided in section 911 wilfully makes a false statement in the report, it is subject to an additional penalty of $1,000.00.

450.2932 Prohibited conduct as misdemeanor; fine.
Sec. 932.

(1) A person shall not knowingly make or file or knowingly assist in the making or filing of a false or fraudulent report, certificate, or other statement that a domestic or foreign corporation is required to file under this act with a public officer of this state, and a person that knows that a report, certificate or statement is false or fraudulent, shall not procure, counsel or advise the making or filing of that report, certificate, or statement. A person that violates this subsection is guilty of a misdemeanor punishable by a fine of not more than $1,000.00 for each violation of this subsection.

(2) An officer or agent of a corporation shall not knowingly falsify or wrongfully alter the books, records, or accounts of a corporation. An officer or agent that violates this subsection is guilty of a misdemeanor punishable by a fine of not more than $1,000.00 for each violation of this subsection.

Chapter 10 – Foreign Corporations

450.3001 Foreign corporation authorized to conduct affairs in this state on January 1, 1983; rights and privileges; duties, restrictions, penalties, and liabilities.
Sec. 1001.

A foreign corporation that was authorized to conduct affairs in this state on January 1, 1983, for a purpose for which a corporation might secure authority to conduct affairs in this state under this act, has the rights and privileges applicable to a foreign corporation that receives a certificate of authority to conduct affairs in this state under this act. Beginning on January 1, 1983, the corporation is subject to the duties, restrictions, penalties, and liabilities under this act that are applicable to a foreign corporation that receives a certificate of authority to conduct affairs in this state under this act.

450.3002 Foreign corporation receiving certificate of authority under act; rights and privileges; duties, restrictions, penalties, and liabilities.
Sec. 1002.

(1) A foreign corporation that receives a certificate of authority under this act, until a certificate of revocation or of withdrawal is issued under this act, has the same rights and privileges as a domestic corporation organized for the purposes contained in the application under which the certificate of authority is issued. Except as otherwise provided in this act, the corporation is subject to the same duties, restrictions, penalties, and liabilities of a similar domestic corporation.

(2) This act does not authorize this state to regulate the organization or internal affairs of a foreign corporation authorized to transact business in this state.

450.3003 Foreign corporation conducting affairs without certificate of authority; duties, restrictions, penalties, and liabilities.
Sec. 1003.

A foreign corporation which conducts affairs in this state without a certificate of authority under this act is subject to the same duties, restrictions, penalties, and liabilities now or hereafter imposed upon a foreign corporation which receives such certificate of authority, in addition to any other penalty or liability imposed by law.

450.3011 Foreign corporation; certificate of authority required; extent of authorization to conduct affairs in state.
Sec. 1011.

A foreign corporation shall not conduct affairs in this state until it has procured a certificate of authority so to do from the administrator. A foreign corporation may be authorized to conduct affairs in this state which may be conducted lawfully in this state by a domestic corporation, to the extent that it is authorized to conduct such affairs in the jurisdiction where it is organized, but no other affairs.

450.3012 Foreign corporation not considered to be conducting affairs in state; activities; applicability of section.
Sec. 1012.

(1) Without excluding other activities that may not constitute conducting affairs in this state, a foreign corporation is not considered to be conducting affairs in this state for the purposes of this act solely because it is carrying on in this state any 1 or more of the following activities:
(a) Maintaining, defending, or settling any proceeding.

   (b) Holding meetings of the board of directors, shareholders, or members or carrying on other activities concerning internal corporate affairs.

   (c) Maintaining bank accounts.

   (d) Maintaining offices or agencies for the transfer, exchange, or registration of the corporation's own securities or maintaining trustees or depositories with respect to those securities.

   (e) Selling through independent contractors.

   (f) Soliciting or obtaining orders, whether by mail or through employees or agents or otherwise, if the orders require acceptance outside this state before they become contracts.

   (g) Soliciting or obtaining donations, whether by mail, by telephone or other form of remote communications, by electronic transmission, or through employees, agents, volunteers or otherwise, if the donations are made to a foreign corporation that has its principal place of business outside the state.

   (h) Creating or acquiring indebtedness, mortgages, or security interests in real or personal property.

   (i) Securing or collecting debts or enforcing mortgages and security interests in property that secures those debts.

   (j) Owning, without more, real or personal property.

   (k) Conducting an isolated transaction that is completed within 30 days and that is not 1 transaction in the course of repeated transactions of a similar nature.

   (l) Transacting business in interstate commerce.

(2) This section does not apply in determining the contracts or activities that may subject a foreign corporation to service of process or taxation in this state or to regulation under any other statute of this state.

450.3013 Acquisition of federally insured or guaranteed loan by foreign corporation.
Sec. 1013.

(1) A foreign corporation may acquire, or through another person entitled to conduct affairs or transact business in this state may make, a loan that is insured or guaranteed in whole or in part by the federal department of housing and urban development, department of veteran's affairs, or a successor or other agency of the federal government and that is secured in whole or in part by 1 or more mortgages of real property that is located in this state, and a foreign corporation may purchase a loan that is secured in whole or in part by a mortgage of real property that is located in this state, without maintaining authority to conduct affairs in this state under this act or any other law of this state that relates to qualification or maintaining authority to conduct affairs in this state and without paying a fee to qualify or maintain that authority to conduct affairs in this state.

(2) A failure of a foreign corporation described in subsection (1) to qualify or maintain authority to conduct affairs in this state under this act or a failure to pay fees to qualify or maintain authority to conduct affairs in this state

does not affect or impair its ownership of a loan or its right to collect and
service the loan through another person that is entitled to conduct affairs or
transact business in this state, or its right to enforce a loan or to acquire,
hold, protect, convey, lease, or otherwise contract and deal with respect to
any property mortgaged as security for the loan.
(3) As used in this section, "loan" includes an interest or participation in a loan.

450.3015 Application of foreign corporation for certificate of authority to conduct affairs in state; contents.
Sec. 1015.

To procure a certificate of authority to conduct affairs in this state, a foreign
corporation shall file with the administrator an application that contains all of
the following:
    (a) The name of the corporation and the jurisdiction of its incorporation.
    (b) The date of incorporation and the period of duration of the corporation.
    (c) The street address, and the mailing address if it is different from the
        street address, of its main business or headquarters office.
    (d) The street address of its registered office in this state, the mailing
        address if it is different from the street address, and the name of its
        resident agent in this state at that address, together with a statement that
        the resident agent is an agent of the corporation on which process
        against the corporation may be served.
    (e) The character of the affairs it is to conduct in this state, together with a
        statement that it is authorized to conduct those affairs in the jurisdiction
        of its incorporation.
    (f) Any additional information that the administrator reasonably requires
        in order to determine whether the corporation is entitled to a certificate
        of authority to conduct affairs in this state and to determine the fees and
        taxes prescribed by law.

450.3016 Application of foreign corporation to conduct affairs in state; certificate; attachment; fees; issuance of certificate; duration of authority.
Sec. 1016.

(1) A foreign corporation shall attach a certificate to an application for
authority to conduct affairs in this state under section 1015 that states that
the corporation is in good standing under the laws of the jurisdiction of its
incorporation, is executed by the official of the jurisdiction who has custody
of the records that pertain to corporations, and is dated not more than 30
days before the date the application is filed. If the certificate is in a foreign
language, the foreign corporation shall attach a translation of the certificate
under oath of the translator to the certificate.
(2) If a foreign corporation files an application described in subsection (1),
accompanied by the filing and franchise fees prescribed by law, the
administrator shall issue to the foreign corporation a certificate of authority

to conduct affairs in this state. When a certificate of authority is issued, the foreign corporation is authorized to conduct in this state any affairs of the character set forth in its application that a domestic corporation formed under this act may lawfully transact. The authority granted under this subsection continues so long as the foreign corporation retains its authority to conduct its affairs in the jurisdiction of its incorporation and its authority to conduct affairs in this state is not surrendered, suspended, or revoked.

450.3021 Foreign corporation authorized to conduct affairs in state; filing with administrator copy of amended application; contents; survivor of merger or conversion.
Sec. 1021.

(1) Except as otherwise provided in this section, a foreign corporation authorized to conduct affairs in this state that changes its corporate name, or enlarges, limits, or otherwise changes the affairs that the foreign corporation proposes to conduct in this state, or makes any other change that affects the information included in its application for certificate of authority to conduct affairs in this state, shall file an amended application with the administrator within 30 days after the time a change becomes effective. A foreign corporation may make a change in its registered office or resident agent under section 242. An amended application under this subsection shall state all of the following:
   (a) The name of the foreign corporation as it appears on the records of the administrator and the jurisdiction of its incorporation.
   (b) The date the foreign corporation was authorized to conduct affairs in this state.
   (c) If the name of the foreign corporation has changed, a statement of the name relinquished, a statement of the new name, and a statement that the name was properly changed under the laws of the jurisdiction of its incorporation and the date the name was changed.
   (d) If the affairs that the foreign corporation proposes to conduct in this state enlarge, limit, or otherwise change the affairs the foreign corporation is authorized to conduct, a statement reflecting the change and a statement that the foreign corporation is authorized to conduct in the jurisdiction of its incorporation the affairs that it proposes to conduct in this state.
   (e) Any additional information as the administrator may require.
(2) If a foreign corporation that is authorized to conduct affairs in this state is the survivor of a merger permitted by the laws of the jurisdiction in which the foreign corporation is incorporated, within 30 days after the merger becomes effective, the foreign corporation shall file a certificate that is issued by the proper officer of the jurisdiction of its incorporation and attests to the occurrence of the merger. If the merger has changed the corporate name of the foreign corporation, or has enlarged, limited, or changed the affairs that the foreign corporation proposes to conduct in this

state, or changed any of the information included in the application, the foreign corporation shall comply with subsection (1).

(3) If a foreign corporation that is authorized to conduct affairs in this state is the survivor of a conversion under the laws of the jurisdiction in which the foreign corporation is incorporated, the foreign corporation shall, within 30 days after the conversion becomes effective, file a certificate that is issued by the proper officers of the jurisdiction of its incorporation and attests to the occurrence of the conversion. If the conversion has changed the corporate name of the foreign corporation, or has enlarged, limited, or changed the affairs the foreign corporation that proposes to conduct in this state or has affected the information included in the application, the foreign corporation shall comply with subsection (1).

450.3031 Foreign corporation authorized to conduct affairs in state; withdrawal; certificate; application.
Sec. 1031.

A foreign corporation authorized to conduct affairs in this state may withdraw from this state upon receiving from the administrator a certificate of withdrawal. The foreign corporation shall file an application for withdrawal setting forth:

(a) The name of the corporation and the jurisdiction of its incorporation.
(b) That the corporation is not conducting affairs in this state.
(c) That the corporation surrenders its authority to conduct affairs in this state.

450.3032 Issuance of certificate of withdrawal to foreign corporation; conditions; effect.
Sec. 1032.

If a foreign corporation files an application for withdrawal and pays the filing fees prescribed by law, the administrator shall issue to the foreign corporation a certificate of withdrawal, and both of the following shall occur:

(a) The authority of the foreign corporation to conduct affairs in this state is terminated.
(b) The authority of its resident agent in this state to accept service of process against the foreign corporation is revoked.

450.3035 Foreign corporation authorized to conduct affairs in state; dissolution; termination or cancellation of authority or existence; merger, conversion, or consolidation; filing information, certificate, order, or judgment with administrator; payment of fees; certificate of withdrawal.
Sec. 1035.

(1) If a foreign corporation that is authorized to conduct affairs in this state is dissolved, or its authority or existence is otherwise terminated or canceled

in the jurisdiction of its incorporation, or it is merged into, converted into, or consolidated with another corporation, or business organization, the foreign corporation or business organization shall file with the administrator any information that is required by the administrator to determine and assess any unpaid fees payable by the foreign corporation as required by law and either of the following:

(a) A certificate of the official of the jurisdiction of incorporation of the foreign corporation who has custody of the records pertaining to corporations, evidencing the occurrence of the event.

(b) A certified copy of an order or judgment of a court of competent jurisdiction directing dissolution of the foreign corporation, the termination of its existence, or the cancellation of its authority.

(2) If a foreign corporation files a certificate, order, or judgment under subsection (1) and pays the filing fee prescribed by law, the administrator shall issue a certificate of withdrawal that has the same effect as a certificate of withdrawal under section 1032.

450.3041 Revocation of certificate of authority of foreign corporation to conduct affairs in state; grounds.
Sec. 1041.

In addition to any other ground for revocation provided by law, the administrator may revoke the certificate of authority of a foreign corporation to conduct affairs in this state, in the manner described in section 1042, on any of the following grounds:

(a) The corporation fails to maintain a resident agent in this state as required under this act.

(b) The corporation, after changing its registered office or resident agent, fails to file a statement of the change as required under this act.

(c) The corporation fails to file an amended application if required under this act.

(d) The corporation, after becoming the survivor in a merger, consolidation, or conversion, fails to file a certificate that attests to the occurrence of the merger, consolidation, or conversion as required under this act.

(e) The corporation fails to file its annual report within the time required under this act, or fails to pay an annual fee required under this act.

450.3042 Revocation of certificate of authority of foreign corporation to conduct affairs in state; notice of default; certificate of revocation; force and effect.
Sec. 1042.

(1) The administrator shall revoke a certificate of authority of a foreign corporation only if he or she gives the foreign corporation at least 90 days' notice, by mail or by electronic transmission under subsection (2), that a

default under section 1041 exists and that he or she will revoke its certificate of authority unless the default is cured within 90 days after the notice is mailed or electronically transmitted, and the corporation fails within the 90-day period to cure the default.

(2) The administrator may electronically transmit a notice described in subsection (1) to the resident agent of the corporation in the manner authorized by the corporation.

(3) If he or she revokes a certificate of authority under this section, the administrator shall issue a certificate of revocation and shall mail, or if authorized by the corporation, may electronically transmit, a copy of the certificate of revocation to the resident agent of the corporation.

(4) Issuing a certificate of revocation under this section has the same force and effect as issuing a certificate of withdrawal under section 1031.

450.3051 Action commenced by foreign corporation without certificate of authority prohibited; order of dismissal; effect of failure to obtain certificate of authority on validity of contract and act of corporation; defense of action or proceeding.
Sec. 1051.

(1) A foreign corporation that conducts affairs in this state without a certificate of authority shall not maintain an action or proceeding in any court of this state until the corporation obtains a certificate of authority. An action commenced by a foreign corporation that does not have a certificate of authority shall not be dismissed if the foreign corporation obtains a certificate of authority before the order of dismissal. If an action or proceeding is dismissed because a foreign corporation does not have a certificate of authority, the order of dismissal shall be without prejudice to the recommencement of the action or proceeding by the foreign corporation after it obtains a certificate of authority. This subsection applies to the foreign corporation and to any of the following:

   (a) A successor in interest of the foreign corporation, except a receiver, trustee in bankruptcy, or other representative of creditors of the corporation.

   (b) An assignee of the foreign corporation, except an assignee for value that accepts an assignment without knowledge that the foreign corporation should have but did not obtain a certificate of authority in this state.

(2) Failure of a foreign corporation to obtain a certificate of authority to conduct affairs in this state does not impair the validity of a contract or act of the corporation, and does not prevent the corporation from defending an action or proceeding in a court of this state.

450.3055 Foreign corporation conducting affairs in state without certificate of authority; penalty.
Sec. 1055.

In addition to any other liability imposed by law, a foreign corporation conducting affairs in this state without a certificate of authority shall forfeit to the state a penalty of not less than $100.00 nor more than $1,000.00 for each calendar month, not more than 5 years prior thereto, in which it has conducted affairs in this state without a certificate of authority. This penalty shall not exceed $10,000.00. The penalty shall be recovered with costs in an action prosecuted by the attorney general.

450.3060 Fees; payment; certification of file or record; waiver; form of payment; "armed forces" defined.
Sec. 1060.

(1) When delivering a document described in this subsection to the administrator for filing, the person shall pay the administrator whichever of the following fees apply to that document:
   (a) Articles of incorporation of a domestic corporation, $10.00.
   (b) An application of a foreign corporation for a certificate of authority to conduct affairs in this state, $10.00.
   (c) An amendment to the articles of incorporation of a domestic corporation, $10.00.
   (d) An amended application for certificate of authority to conduct affairs in this state, $10.00.
   (e) A certificate of merger or conversion under chapter 7, $50.00.
   (f) A certificate attesting to the occurrence of a merger of a foreign corporation under section 1021, $10.00.
   (g) A certificate of dissolution, $10.00.
   (h) An application for withdrawal and issuance of a certificate of withdrawal of a foreign corporation, $10.00.
   (i) An application for reservation of corporate name, $10.00.
   (j) A certificate of assumed name or certificate of termination of assumed name, $10.00.
   (k) A statement of change of registered office or resident agent, $5.00.
   (l) Restated articles of incorporation of a domestic corporation, $10.00.
   (m) A certificate of abandonment, $10.00.
   (n) A certificate of correction, $10.00.
   (o) A certificate of revocation of dissolution proceedings, $10.00.
   (p) A certificate of renewal of corporate existence, $10.00.
   (q) For examining a special report required by law, $2.00.
   (r) A certificate of registration of corporate name of a foreign corporation, $50.00.
   (s) A certificate of renewal of registration of corporate name of a foreign corporation, $50.00.

(t) A certificate of termination of registration of corporate name of a foreign corporation, $10.00.

(u) For filing a report required under section 911, $10.00 if paid after September 30, 2019. Before October 1, 2019, the fee is $20.00.

(2) The fees described in subsection (1) are in addition to any franchise fees prescribed under this act. The administrator shall not refund all or any part of a fee described in this section.

(3) Except as provided in subsection (8), the administrator shall deposit all fees received and collected under this section in the state treasury to the credit of the administrator, who may only use the money credited pursuant to legislative appropriation and only in carrying out those duties of the department required by law.

(4) A person shall pay a minimum charge of $1.00 for each certificate and 50 cents per folio to the administrator for certifying a part of a file or record pertaining to a corporation if a fee for that service is not described in subsection (1). The administrator may furnish copies of documents, reports, and papers required or permitted by law to be filed with the administrator, and shall charge for those copies the fee established in a schedule of fees adopted by the administrator with the approval of the state administrative board. The administrator shall retain the revenue collected under this subsection, and the department shall use it to defray the costs for its copying and certifying services.

(5) The administrator shall waive the fee for filing initial articles of incorporation, otherwise required under subsection (1), if a majority of the initial members of a membership corporation, initial directors of a directorship corporation, or initial shareholders of a stock corporation, as applicable, are, or if applicable the initial members, initial directors, or initial shareholders will be, individuals who served in the armed forces and were separated from that service with an honorable character of service or under honorable conditions (general) character of service.

(6) To request a fee waiver under subsection (5), the person that is submitting the document for filing shall submit both of the following to the administrator with the document:

(a) A signed affidavit requesting the fee waiver and certifying that a majority of the initial members of the membership corporation, initial directors of the directorship corporation, or initial shareholders of the stock corporation, as applicable, are, or if applicable the initial members, initial directors, or initial shareholders will be, individuals who served in the armed forces and were separated from that service with an honorable character of service or under honorable conditions (general) character of service.

(b) Copies of form DD214 or form DD215, or any other form that is satisfactory to the department, for each individual described in subsection (5) who is or will be an initial member of the corporation, initial director of the corporation, or initial shareholder of the corporation, as applicable.

(7) If a person pays a fee or penalty on behalf of a domestic or foreign corporation by check and the check is dishonored, the fee is unpaid and the administrator shall rescind the filing of all related documents.

(8) The administrator may accept a credit card in lieu of cash or check as payment of a fee under this act. The administrator shall determine which credit cards he or she shall accept for payment.

(9) The administrator may charge a nonrefundable fee of up to $50.00 for any document submitted or certificate sent by facsimile or electronic transmission. The administrator shall retain the revenue collected under this subsection and the department shall use it in carrying out its duties required by law.

(10) As used in this section, "armed forces" means that term as defined in section 2 of the veteran right to employment services act, 1994 PA 39, MCL 35.1092.

450.3061 Fee for privilege of exercising franchises in state.
Sec. 1061.

Every corporation organized or conducting affairs in this state shall, upon filing its articles, or, if a foreign corporation, upon filing its application for admission, pay to the administrator a fee of $10.00 for the privilege of exercising its franchises within this state, upon such organization or admission as the case may be.

450.3098 Repeal of acts and parts of acts.
Sec. 1098.

The following acts and parts of acts are repealed:
  (a) Act No. 213 of the Public Acts of 1935, being sections 450.401 to 450.402 of the Compiled Laws of 1970.
  (b) Act No. 90 of the Public Acts of 1954, being sections 450.441 to 450.442 of the Compiled Laws of 1970.
  (c) Sections 62, 63, 64, 81, 92, 117, 118, 119, 119a, 120, 121, 122, 123, 124, 124a, 125, 126, 127, 128, 129, 130, 131, 132, 132a, 163, 164, 165, 166, 167, 168, 188, and 189 of Act No. 327 of the Public Acts of 1931, as amended, being sections 450.62, 450.63, 450.64, 450.81, 450.92, 450.117, 450.118, 450.119, 450.119a, 450.120, 450.121, 450.122, 450.123, 450.124, 450.124a, 450.125, 450.126, 450.127, 450.128, 450.129, 450.130, 450.131, 450.132, 450.132a, 450.163, 450.164, 450.165, 450.166, 450.167, 450.168, 450.188, and 450.189 of the Compiled Laws of 1970.
  (d) Act No. 161 of the Public Acts of 1947, being sections 450.421 to 450.422 of the Compiled Laws of 1970.

450.3099 Effective date of act.
Sec. 1099.

This act shall take effect January 1, 1983.

Chapter 11 - Cooperatives

450.3100 Short title.
Sec. 1100.

This chapter shall be known and may be cited as the "consumer cooperative act".

450.3101 Applicability of act and chapter; amendment of articles or bylaws; exemption.
Sec. 1101.

(1) Except as otherwise provided in this act or by other law, this act and this chapter apply to:
  (a) All consumer cooperatives which are organized after the effective date of this amendatory act.
  (b) All consumer cooperatives which have been organized under this act, a predecessor act, or other act and which have represented themselves to be cooperatives.
  (c) All other corporations that elect to accept this act pursuant to section 1192.
  (d) All other cooperatives organized under this chapter.
  (e) All foreign cooperatives to the extent provided in sections 1123 and 1191.
(2) A consumer cooperative which was organized under a predecessor or other act is subject to this act and this chapter except to the extent that either conflicts with the articles, bylaws, or cooperative plan of the consumer cooperative lawfully made pursuant to the predecessor or other act. The consumer cooperative may amend its articles or bylaws to bring itself in conformity with this act. If a corporation elects to accept this act and this chapter pursuant to section 1192, the corporation shall amend its articles and bylaws, as necessary, to bring itself in conformity with this act and this chapter.
(3) A nonprofit power corporation as described in section 261(4) may elect to be exempted from this chapter by the effective date of this amendatory act by a resolution of the board of directors of the corporation. If such a corporation should subsequently elect to accept this act and this chapter pursuant to section 1192, the corporation shall amend its articles and bylaws, as necessary, to bring itself in conformity with this act and this chapter.

(4) This chapter shall not apply to a cooperative organized substantially for the purpose of agricultural production, processing, supply, research, bargaining, or marketing which is organized under sections 98 to 109 of Act No. 327 of the Public Acts of 1931, being sections 450.98 to 450.109 of the Michigan Compiled Laws, or a farm cooperative the majority of votes of which are held by farmers, unless the cooperative elects to accept this chapter pursuant to section 1192.

450.3102 Controlling definitions.
Sec. 1102.

The definitions contained in sections 1103 and 1104 shall control in the interpretation of this chapter, unless the context otherwise requires.

450.3103 Definitions; C to F.
Sec. 1103.

(1) "Consumer" means a natural person who acquires, or commits to acquire in the future from the cooperative primarily for consumption, use, or occupancy by the person or the person's family, any of the goods, services, or facilities furnished by the cooperative.
(2) "Consumer cooperative" means a cooperative the majority of the votes of which are held by consumers, or, in the case of a cooperative which provides residential dwelling units, the majority of the votes of which are held by consumers and the majority of members of which do not have the right of possession or occupancy of dwelling units they do not occupy.
(3) "Cooperative" means a corporation organized on a cooperative basis or similar basis that is provided in law as a criterion for being a cooperative.
(4) "Cooperative basis" means:
  (a) That, subject to section 1133, each member has 1 vote, except as provided in this chapter.
  (b) That the dividends, if any, paid on member capital do not exceed 8% per year.
  (c) That the net savings are distributed as provided in section 1135.
  (d) That business is engaged in for the mutual benefit of its members.
(5) "Electronic transmission" or "electronically transmitted" means any form of communication that meets all of the following:
  (a) It does not directly involve the physical transmission of paper.
  (b) It creates a record that may be retained and retrieved by the recipient.
  (c) It may be directly reproduced in paper form by the recipient through an automated process.
(6) "Foreign cooperative" means a corporation organized under laws other than the laws of this state operating on a cooperative basis or a similar basis that is provided in those other laws as a criterion for being a cooperative.

450.3104 Definitions; I to U.
Sec. 1104.

As used in this chapter:
- (a) "Insolvent" means being unable to pay debts as they become due in the usual course of a debtor's business.
- (b) "Member capital" means the assets that a member must provide by payment, transfer, or allocation of net savings to a cooperative as a condition of admission to or retention of membership and with respect to which the member has rights to dividends, redemption, or distributions on dissolution under this chapter.
- (c) "Membership fee" means a nonredeemable fee that a member must pay to a cooperative as a condition of admission to or retention of membership in the cooperative that is not member capital or a fee for goods, services, or facilities.
- (d) "Patron" means a person whose economic exchange is a regular part of the business of a cooperative or foreign cooperative, if the economic exchange is the same type of regular economic exchange engaged in by any class of members.
- (e) "Patronage" means the selling or providing of goods, services, or facilities to, or the buying of goods, services, or facilities from members or other persons, or providing labor or services to or by a cooperative.
- (f) "Redemption" means any method by which a cooperative exchanges cash or debt instruments for member capital, including, but not limited to, repurchase, redemption, refund, or repayment.
- (g) "Referendum" means a method of member voting that utilizes secret ballot and established polling places as provided in the cooperative's bylaws or under section 409.
- (h) "Unincorporated cooperative" means either of the following:
  - (i) An association of 2 or more persons that is organized on a cooperative basis and that is not a corporation.
  - (ii) An association of 2 or more persons that is organized under the laws of another state and operates on either a cooperative basis or a similar basis provided in that state as the criterion for being a cooperative, and that is not a corporation.

450.3107 Inconsistent provisions inapplicable to chapter.
Sec. 1107.

To the extent that sections 301(4) and 301(5), 855, and 901 are inconsistent with this chapter, they shall not apply to cooperatives.

450.3109 Requirements of MCL 460.1 et seq. not modified; effect of economic activity conducted by cooperative.
Sec. 1109.

(1) This chapter does not modify the requirements of Act No. 3 of the Public Acts of 1939, being sections 460.1 to 460.8 of the Michigan Compiled Laws.
(2) The fact that a cooperative conducts economic activity under this act shall not alone cause the economic activity of the cooperative to be considered a conspiracy or combination in restraint of trade or an illegal monopoly, or an attempt to lessen competition or fix prices arbitrarily.

450.3121 Articles of incorporation; requirement.
Sec. 1121.

In addition to the requirements of section 202, the articles of incorporation of a cooperative organized under this act shall state whether the cooperative will be financed on a membership fee basis, a member capital basis, or a combination of both.

450.3123 Use of term "cooperative,""co-op,""consumer cooperative," or any variation thereof.
Sec. 1123.

(1) The term "cooperative", "co-op", or any variation thereof, may only be used in the name of cooperatives organized under or subject to this chapter, corporations organized under or subject to sections 98 to 109 of Act No. 327 of the Public Acts of 1931, being sections 450.98 to 450.109 of the Michigan Compiled Laws, parent cooperative preschools licensed under Act No. 116 of the Public Acts of 1973, being sections 722.111 to 722.128 of the Michigan Compiled Laws, credit unions chartered under the laws of this state or federal law, corporations organized on a cooperative basis or similar basis and organized before the effective date of this amendatory act as nonprofit corporations, unincorporated cooperatives, foreign cooperatives, any entities wholly owned by any of the foregoing or any combination of such entities, and any other entities specifically authorized by statute to use "cooperative", "co-op", or any variation thereof.
(2) The term "consumer cooperative" or any variation thereof may only be used in the name of a consumer cooperative or a foreign or unincorporated cooperative the majority of the votes of which are held by consumers and which complies with sections 1132 and 1138.
(3) Unless authorized by subsection (1) or (2), or as otherwise specifically provided by law, a person shall not use the term "cooperative", "co-op", "consumer cooperative", or any variation thereof, as part of a corporate or other business name or title.

(4) This section shall not be construed to authorize any use of the term "co-op", "cooperative", "consumer cooperative", or any variation thereof, that is prohibited by the cooperative identity protection act.

450.3125 Adoption of initial bylaws; ratification or amendment; contents of bylaws.
Sec. 1125.

(1) Notwithstanding section 231, the initial bylaws of a cooperative may be adopted by the incorporators, the board, or the members. If initial bylaws are adopted by the incorporators or the board, at the first meeting of members the bylaws shall be submitted to the members for ratification or amendment.
(2) Bylaws may contain provisions for educational programs for directors, members, employees, patrons, prospective members, and the community and provisions for cooperative relations with cooperatives and unincorporated cooperatives.

450.3131 Organization on nonstock membership basis.
Sec. 1131.

Notwithstanding section 302, a cooperative organized under this act shall be organized on a nonstock membership basis and shall not be organized on a stock or directorship basis.

450.3132 Membership; notice of qualifications.
Sec. 1132.

Subject to section 304(7), membership in a consumer cooperative subject to this act shall be available to all patrons of the cooperative who are consumers. The bylaws may make membership available to other patrons. For any other cooperative, 50% or more of the patronage shall be with members or, subject to section 304(7), membership shall be available to all patrons. All cooperatives shall give all patrons reasonable notice of the qualifications for membership.

450.3133 Classification.
Sec. 1133.

If a cooperative has classes of members pursuant to section 304, classification shall be based only on 1 or more of the following number of members, number of persons served, type of patronage, level of patronage, or whether or not members are patrons. In a consumer cooperative, classification of consumers by level of patronage shall not be used.

450.3134 Cooperative organized on member capital basis, member fee basis, or basis combining member capital and membership fee; powers.
Sec. 1134.

(1) A cooperative which is organized on a member capital basis or on a basis combining member capital and membership fee may provide for any of the following, if such provision is set forth in the articles or bylaws:
   (a) A maximum member capital to be held by any 1 member.
   (b) Transfer of member capital pursuant to section 304(6).
   (c) Mandatory contribution or contributions of member capital as a condition or conditions of admission to or retention of membership, including but not limited to initial capital contributions, surcharges, and distributions of net savings pursuant to section 1135.
   (d) A dividend on membership capital, not to exceed 8% per year.
   (e) Special assessments on members.
(2) A cooperative which is organized on a membership fee basis or on a basis combining member capital and membership fee may provide for either or both of the following as a condition or conditions of admission to or retention of membership in the cooperative, if such a provision is set forth in its articles or bylaws:
   (a) The charging of a nonredeemable initial or periodic membership fee or fees.
   (b) Nonredeemable special assessments on members.

450.3135 Net savings; determination, allocation, distribution, and use; apportionment of losses.
Sec. 1135.

(1) At least once each year, a cooperative shall determine its net savings by deducting from total income:
   (a) All operating costs and expenses.
   (b) Reasonable reserves for depreciation and obsolescence of property, doubtful accounts, other valuation or operating reserves, capital investments and reserves for capital investment.
   (c) Dividends paid on member capital and interest or dividends paid on nonvoting investment certificates or bonds, if any.
(2) The articles or bylaws may provide for any reasonable method of allocating net savings by the board of directors for the common benefit of all the patrons of a cooperative.
(3) Unless the articles or bylaws otherwise provide pursuant to subsection (2), net savings shall be allocated, distributed, or used in any of the following ways:
   (a) By allocation of net savings to all patrons at a uniform rate in proportion to their individual patronage, provided that different rates of allocation may be established according to the net savings generated by various departments or types of business done by the cooperative. Distribution to patrons may be made as follows:

(i) In cash or credits. Credits shall be evidenced by shares, revolving fund certificates, notices of allocation, capital credits, or other certificates or notices of the cooperative, or any combination thereof.

(ii) In the case of nonmember patrons who have subscribed for membership, distribution may be credited toward payment of unpaid member capital or membership fees.

(iii) In the case of nonmember patrons, distribution of the proportionate amount of net savings generated by nonmember patronage may be made to a general fund. Redistribution shall be made to an individual nonmember patron only upon request and presentation of evidence of the nonmember's patronage. Such net savings may be distributed in cash or credited toward payment of member capital or membership fees. Reasonable notice shall be provided to nonmember patrons of their rights to redistribution and the means of applying for membership.

(b) By allocation to retained earnings, operating costs or capital expenditures of the cooperative to reduce the costs of goods, facilities, or services, to improve the quality provided or otherwise to further the common benefit of the patrons.

(4) The articles or bylaws may include any reasonable provisions for the apportionment of losses.

450.3136 Certificate; issuance; contents; restrictions on dividends.
Sec. 1136.

(1) If a cooperative is to be financed in whole or in part on a member capital basis, each member shall be provided a certificate or certificates setting forth the initial member capital of the member.

(2) A certificate issued pursuant to this section shall contain the information required by section 1138. The certificate may be denominated a membership certificate, share certificate, stock certificate, or a similar designation but shall not constitute shares as defined in section 109.

(3) The board of directors shall not pay dividends when currently the cooperative is insolvent or would thereby be made insolvent, or when the declaration, payment, or distribution of a dividend would be contrary to the articles or bylaws.

450.3137 Nonvoting investment certificate or bond.
Sec. 1137.

Subject to the uniform securities act, 1964 PA 265, MCL 451.501 to 451.818, and the uniform securities act (2002), 2008 PA 551, MCL 451.2101 to 451.2703, a cooperative may offer to its members or to the general public any form of nonvoting investment certificate or bond that may bear interest or dividends as provided by the board of directors.

450.3138 Advising persons in writing; statement on membership certificate.
Sec. 1138.

Prior to accepting a person as a member or any membership fee or member capital, a cooperative shall advise the person in writing of the items in subdivisions (a) to (g). A cooperative shall also conspicuously state on each membership certificate the items in subdivisions (a), (e), and (f):

    (a) A statement that the corporation is a cooperative subject to this act and under what act it is organized.

    (b) A statement that the purpose of becoming a member of a cooperative is to assure access to the goods, services, and facilities of the cooperative and not to gain profit.

    (c) A statement of voting rights and rights to notice of meetings of members.

    (d) A statement of the qualifications for admission to and retention of membership and the right of the cooperative to terminate membership, if any.

    (e) A statement of the restrictions, if any, on the transfer of memberships.

    (f) A statement of the rights to redemption of a member capital, if any, or a statement that member capital is not redeemable.

    (g) A statement of the right of members to call special meetings or cause a mail ballot, to receive annual reports, and to secure other material information concerning the cooperative.

450.3139 Redemption of member capital; failure to patronize cooperative; notice of redemption; failure to respond and claim payment; failure to claim refunds of patronage capital, deposits, and fees; failure of nonmember patron to pay in or accumulate full member capital or comply with bylaws.
Sec. 1139.

(1) Unless the articles or bylaws provide that the member capital is not redeemable, upon termination of a membership issued on a member capital basis, a cooperative shall redeem the member's member capital by paying to the member in cash or other property (i) the lesser of the member's member capital or the member's pro rata share of the total member capital of the cooperative determined according to the ratio each member's member capital bears to total member capital, unless a different proration is provided in the articles; or (ii) such other amount as may be provided in the articles or bylaws. Payment shall be made within 5 years from the date of termination, unless the articles or bylaws provide for a different period for payment.

(2) Unless the articles or bylaws provide that member capital is not redeemable, a cooperative may adopt and implement any plan to partially redeem member capital.

(3) A cooperative shall not redeem member capital or any portion thereof under either of the following conditions:

(a) When the cooperative is insolvent or when the redemption would render the cooperative insolvent.

(b) Unless after redemption there remains outstanding 1 or more classes of members possessing among them, collectively, voting rights.

(4) The articles or bylaws may provide that if a member fails to patronize a cooperative to an extent and within a specific period of time, the membership shall be terminated.

(5) A person entitled to payment for redemption of member capital shall be given reasonable notice of the redemption, which notice may be by mail to the last known address of the person. If the person fails to respond to the notice and claim the payment within 5 years from the date of notice, that person shall have no further rights in the member capital and the member capital may be added to the general funds of the cooperative.

(6) In the case of a nonprofit power corporation as described in section 261(4), any refunds of patronage capital, deposits, and fees of members not claimed within 5 years after reasonable notice has been given to the member's last known address shall remain the property of the corporation. If any such refund is not claimed by the member within the 5-year period, the member shall have no claim to the refund.

(7) The articles or bylaws may provide that if within any time specified in the bylaws or articles any nonmember patron who has subscribed for membership has not paid in or accumulated the full member capital required for membership or has failed to comply with the provisions of the bylaws, if any, concerning admission to membership, any amounts allocated from net savings and credited to the member capital of the nonmember patron may be added to the general funds of the cooperative and thereafter the nonmember patron shall have no further rights therein.

450.3141 Meetings; petitions; signatures; quorum.
Sec. 1141.

Regular meetings of members shall be held at a time and place prescribed in the bylaws but not less than annually. A special meeting of members may be called by the board of directors or by written petition of members. A petition shall state the purpose or purposes for which the meeting is to be called. Unless the bylaws provide for a smaller percent or number, the number of member signatures required for such a petition shall be 10% of the members. Notwithstanding section 415, unless the articles or bylaws provide a greater percentage or number, a quorum shall be 10% of the members or 50 members, whichever is less.

450.3143 Alternative notice of regular meeting.
Sec. 1143.

Instead of the notice required in section 404, written notice of the time, place, and purposes of a regular meeting of members may be given by a means specified in the bylaws and accessible to all members, if the date of regular meeting is established in the bylaws and the notice is made accessible to all members at least 15 days before the meeting.

450.3144 Proxies; voting by mail ballot, referendum, or electronic transmission.
Sec. 1144.

(1) Notwithstanding section 421, there shall be no proxies unless the articles of incorporation or bylaws authorize use of proxies. If the articles of incorporation or bylaws authorize use of proxies, an individual may not vote more than 5 proxies at any meeting.
(2) The articles or bylaws may provide a method by which members may vote on matters submitted to a vote of members by mail ballot, referendum, or electronic transmission.

450.3145 Amendments; affirmative vote of majority.
Sec. 1145.

Notwithstanding section 611(4), 703a(2)(d), 753(4), or 804(6), unless the articles of incorporation provide for a higher vote for passage, amendment of the articles of incorporation, amendment of the bylaws that alters member voting rights or member capital, merger, disposition of all or substantially all of the assets of the corporation, or dissolution require approval by the affirmative vote of a majority of the votes cast by members that are eligible to vote on that matter, and if a class is eligible to vote on that matter as a class, the affirmative vote of a majority of the votes cast by members of that class. An action described in this section shall be taken at a meeting called according to the notice provisions of section 404.

450.3146 Effective date of adopted action; confirmation vote; filing with administrator.
Sec. 1146.

(1) An action subject to the vote requirement of section 1145 shall not take effect for 60 days from the date of adoption and shall be subject to 1 confirmation vote as provided in subsection (2) if the action is adopted by less than a majority of all the members eligible to vote.
(2) If a petition of 15% or more of the members eligible to vote is presented to the cooperative prior to the sixtieth day after the adoption of the action, the cooperative shall cause a confirmation vote to be held. The cooperative shall cause a special meeting or, if authorized, mail ballot or referendum to be conducted within 45 days of receipt of the petition. The confirmation vote must achieve the vote which would have been required for original adoption. If confirmed, the action or amendment may take effect

immediately after the confirmation or upon filing with the administrator, if such filing is required.

(3) If an action or amendment is subject to confirmation, a filing shall not be made with the administrator until the time for presenting a petition has expired or the action is confirmed.

450.3147 Dispute resolution body.
Sec. 1147.

A cooperative may authorize in its articles or bylaws the establishment of a neutral dispute resolution body. The dispute resolution body shall attempt to settle disputes between the cooperative and any of its members. It shall be composed of individuals who are approved by both parties to the dispute, which individuals may be members or nonmembers, but not officers or directors of the cooperative. The bylaws of a cooperative may provide that membership in the cooperative is conditioned upon participation in good faith in the dispute resolution process authorized by this section.

450.3148 Purchase or sale under execution, in course of bankruptcy, or by legal process or operation of law; pledge of certificate; assignment of proprietary lease or other agreement.
Sec. 1148.

(1) The purchase or sale of any member capital or privileges in a cooperative made under execution, or in the course of bankruptcy proceedings, or by any legal process or by operation of law, shall not give any person any membership right, title, or interest in a cooperative, unless in accordance with the articles or bylaws of the cooperative.

(2) No subsequent amendment to the articles or bylaws shall invalidate or otherwise impair a pledge of a certificate issued under section 1136 or an assignment of a proprietary lease or other agreement providing for occupancy of facilities furnished by the cooperative, if the pledge or assignment was made when the articles or bylaws expressly permitted the pledge or assignment in connection with loans made to members.

450.3149 Books for recording operations; annual report, balance sheet, and income statement; certified report of condition; copies of reports; mailings at request and expense of member; notice of member's desire to be contacted by other members regarding proposal.
Sec. 1149.

(1) A cooperative shall keep a set of books for recording its operations. A written report, including a statement of the amount of its transactions with members and the amount of its transactions with nonmember patrons, a balance sheet, and an income statement shall be prepared annually.

(2) A cooperative shall prepare, not later than 120 days after the close of its fiscal year, a report of its condition, which report shall be certified by the president. The report shall include all of the following:

(a) The name and principal address of the cooperative.

(b) The names, addresses, and date of expiration of terms of the officers and directors, and their rate of compensation, if any.

(c) The number of memberships granted and terminated and the amount of member capital paid in during the fiscal year.

(3) A copy of the reports required by this section shall be presented at the annual membership meeting or distributed to each member. Copies of the report shall be kept on file at the principal office of the cooperative and shall be made available to members, subscribers, and applicants for membership during regular business hours. In addition, copies of the report shall be mailed to a member upon written request by the member.

(4) If a membership address list is not accessible to members, then any mailing reasonably related to the affairs of the membership shall be made by a cooperative at the request and expense of a member.

(5) If a member makes a timely request in writing that a cooperative notify the membership of the member's desire to be contacted by other members regarding a proposal then pending for vote by the membership, the cooperative shall include in the next communication sent by the cooperative to all members, if any, a brief notice of that member's request which shall identify the member and shall state whether the member is for or against the proposal and how to contact that member.

450.3151 Initial board of directors; membership; term.
Sec. 1151.

Notwithstanding section 505, the initial board of directors of a cooperative shall consist of at least 5 persons. The term of office of directors shall be no more than 3 years.

450.3152 Board of directors; election or appointment other than by vote of membership.
Sec. 1152.

Notwithstanding section 505, the bylaws of a cooperative may provide for 1/3 or less of the board of directors to be elected or appointed other than by a vote of the membership.

450.3153 Affiliation with another organization; section inapplicable to allocations of net savings.
Sec. 1153.

A vote of the membership shall be required to affiliate with another organization involving the investment of more than 30% of the assets of the cooperative, if the affiliation is not in the usual and regular course of its business. This section shall not apply to any allocations of net savings to the cooperative by any person.

450.3161 Amendment to articles of incorporation; calling special meeting; consideration of proposed amendment.
Sec. 1161.

An amendment to the articles of incorporation may be proposed by the board, by 10% or more of the members, or by some smaller percentage of members established in the articles or bylaws. If proposed by the number of members required for calling a special meeting pursuant to section 1141, a special meeting shall be called within a reasonable time. If proposed by less than the number of members required to call a special meeting, then the proposed amendment shall be considered at the next annual or special meeting.

450.3162 Distribution of assets generally.
Sec. 1162.

In the event of an amendment to the articles of incorporation or bylaws, merger, or disposition of substantially all of the assets of a cooperative, or a dissolution, that results in a distribution of all or substantially all of the assets of the corporation to members, the corporation shall make that distribution in the manner and order provided in section 1183.

450.3183 Distribution of assets upon dissolution; distribution of assets held for charitable or similar purpose; redemption of investment certificates.
Sec. 1183.

(1) Notwithstanding section 855, upon dissolution, the assets of a cooperative shall be distributed in the following manner and order:
   (a) By paying or providing for payment of its debts and expenses.
   (b) By redeeming member capital by paying to the member in cash or other property (i) the lesser of the member's member capital or the member's pro rata share of total member capital of the cooperative determined according to the ratio each member's member capital bears to total member capital, unless a different proration is provided in the articles; or (ii) such other amount as may be provided in the articles or bylaws.

(c) By distributing any surplus to (i) those patrons who have been members or subscribers at any time during not less than the 6 years preceding dissolution or since formation of the cooperative, whichever is less, on the basis of patronage during that period; (ii) any other cooperative, foreign cooperative, or nonprofit organization designated by membership resolution; or (iii) both.

(2) Assets held by a cooperative for a charitable or similar purpose shall be distributed pursuant to section 855(c).

(3) Investment certificates issued pursuant to section 1137 shall be redeemed according to the terms of the certificates.

450.3191 Foreign cooperative.
Sec. 1191.

A foreign cooperative shall be entitled to conduct its affairs in this state upon complying with the provisions of chapter 10 and, if a consumer cooperative, by agreeing to provide its members and patrons residing in this state reasonable notice of their membership rights. Reasonable notice shall be considered given if written notice of the matters required to be disclosed by section 1132 is provided to each patron residing in this state and written notice of the matters required to be disclosed by section 1138 is provided to each member residing in this state.

450.3192 Election by corporation to accept act and chapter; procedure; effect of filing certificate of election.
Sec. 1192.

(1) Any corporation may elect to accept this act and this chapter as follows:
   (a) The board of directors shall adopt a resolution recommending that the corporation accept this act and this chapter and directing that the question of acceptance be submitted to a vote at a meeting of the members or stockholders entitled to vote thereon. Written notice stating that the purpose, or 1 of the purposes, of the meeting is to consider electing to accept this act and this chapter, shall be given to each member and stockholder entitled to vote at the meeting, within the time and in the manner provided in this act for the giving of notice of meetings of members. The election to accept this act and this chapter shall require for adoption that vote which is required by that corporation to amend its articles of incorporation.
   (b) A certificate of election to accept the act and this chapter shall be filed in accordance with section 131. The certificate shall set forth:
      (i) The name of the corporation.
      (ii) A statement by the corporation that it has elected to accept this act and this chapter.
      (iii) A statement setting forth the date of the meeting of members or stockholders at which the election to accept this act and this chapter was made, that a quorum was present at the meeting, and

that the acceptance was authorized by that vote which is required by the corporation to amend its articles of incorporation.

(iv) If the corporation has issued shares of stock, a statement of that fact including the number of shares issued and outstanding, and a statement that all issued and outstanding shares of stock will be canceled upon the filing of the statement and that from and after the effective date of filing the authority of the corporation to issue shares of stock shall be terminated.

(v) A statement of the manner and basis of converting shares or memberships, voting rights, and equity interests into memberships, voting rights, and member capital subject to this chapter.

(2) Upon filing of the certificate of election, the election of the corporation to accept this act and this chapter shall become effective and the corporation shall have the same powers and privileges and be subject to the same duties, restrictions, penalties, and liabilities as though the corporation had been originally organized under this act and this chapter.